Scars of Silence

A JOURNEY THROUGH TRAFFICKING AND SURVIVAL

By

ROSELINE CHINASA OIWOH

Copyright

Copyright © 2025 ROSELINE CHINASA OIWOH

Published by

All rights reserved. No part of this book may be reproduced or transmitted in any form or by any means, electronic or mechanical, including photocopying, recording, or by any information storage and retrieval system, without written permission from the publisher and author.

Dedication

To God Almighty—thank You for being my strength when I had none, and for carrying me through the darkest moments. This story would not exist without Your grace.

To the survivors—your courage, pain, and perseverance are not forgotten. This is for every voice that was silenced, and every soul that found the strength to rise.

And to my husband—your love held me steady when the weight was too heavy. You believed in me, even when I struggled to believe in myself. Thank you, from the deepest part of my heart.

Acknowledgement

I wish to begin by expressing my deepest gratitude to God Almighty, whose strength and grace sustained me throughout the journey of writing this book. It is only through His guidance that this work was made possible.

To my husband, whose unwavering support has been an enduring source of strength—thank you for your steadfast presence, encouragement, and belief in this project. Your role in this journey is both profound and unforgettable.

I extend my sincere appreciation to the editors whose professional insight, thoughtful critique, and careful attention have been instrumental in shaping this manuscript with clarity and integrity.

Finally, I am thankful to all who contributed to this work in any capacity—those who shared their experiences, offered their expertise, or provided encouragement along the way. Your contributions have been invaluable, and I am truly grateful.

Foreword

Every year, countless children around the world fall victim to the horrors of child trafficking. According to the UNODC Report on Human Trafficking (February 2009), *"Globally, almost 20% of all trafficking victims are children. In parts of Africa and the Mekong region, children represent the majority—reaching up to 100% in some areas of West Africa."* The report further highlights that many of these heinous acts occur close to home. In fact, **domestic trafficking** remains the most common form of trafficking in persons.

Roseline, herself a survivor of child trafficking, has written *Scars of Silence: A Journey Through Trafficking and Survival* to give voice to those who have been silenced. Through this book, she shines a light on the lasting scars and silent suffering of victims, particularly children, who have endured the unthinkable.

Rooted in her lived experiences, Roseline bravely shares her own story—offering readers a deeply personal and moving account of survival. Her journey is one marked by faith, grace, resilience, and unwavering determination. Through prayer, courage, and hard work, she not only survived but emerged stronger and more empowered. Her life stands as proof that, no matter the darkness, healing and hope are possible.

This book is a compelling reminder that child trafficking is not just a distant tragedy. It can happen anywhere—within homes, communities, and often at the hands of those closest to the victim.

As I read *Scars of Silence*, I found myself completely immersed. The raw honesty, the pain, and the strength woven through each chapter left a lasting impression.

This is not just a story of pain—it's a story of resilience, courage, and ultimately, triumph. It is a book that educates, inspires, and challenges us to confront the brutal realities of child trafficking.

I wholeheartedly recommend *Scars of Silence: A Journey Through Trafficking and Survival* to every reader. It is powerful, necessary, and unforgettable.

- Love-Jane Dick-Onuzuruike

Table of Contents

Chapter 1: Beginnings 1

Chapter 2: Lessons at Home 8

Chapter 3: First Responsibilities 17

Chapter 4: The Journey That Chose Me 28

Chapter 5: A Life of Silence... 32

Chapter 6: The Day I Was Seen 47

Chapter 7: The Lie That Changed Everything 53

Chapter 8: Sent Away Without a Word 58

Chapter 9: A Place That Felt Like Home 66

Chapter 10: Whispers of the Stream............................. 70

Chapter 11: A New Beginning… or So I Thought 75

Chapter 12: Behind Her Smile.. 81

Chapter 13: The House of Broken Promises 87

Chapter 14: Crossing Borders, Carrying Burdens 93

Chapter 16: The Endless Cycle..................................... 109

Chapter 17: The Night I Fought Back 111

Chapter 18: The Voice That Found Me...................... 117

Chapter 19: A Valley Encounter 121

Chapter 20: Secrets and Confidants 126

Chapter 21: Growing Pains... 132

Chapter 22: Trials and Triumphs 140

Chapter 23: Miracles and Meaning............................. 145

Chapter 24: Coming of Age 152

Chapter 25: Looking Back, Moving Forward 159

Author Biography 168
Resources & Support 169

Chapter 1

Beginnings

Why I Had to Speak: A Story of Trafficking and Escape

For years, I have carried the weight of my story, feeling it pressing against my heart, urging me to give it voice. Each year, I promised myself I would write it down, but life's demands swept me along. Now, I am grateful to have finally begun this journey of remembrance, truth, and encouragement. Natalie Goldberg once said, *"We are important and our lives are important, magnificent really, and their details are worthy to be recorded."* I believe this deeply. Our stories are the fabric of our existence—each thread unique, each pattern telling of joys, sorrows, hopes, and victories.

From the title of this book, you may already sense the direction of my story. Yet, every story is different—unique as a fingerprint—shaped by the contours of each person's experience. My reason for speaking is simple yet profound: I want my story to be a source of encouragement and a testament that faith and hope in God's word, along with perseverance, can carry us through the darkest valleys.

Trafficking is not a new word, especially in places like the United Kingdom, Italy, the United States, and beyond. The stories are often traumatic, emotionally draining, and painfully real. Sadly, the number of those trafficked continues to rise each day. I was once a victim of child trafficking. Somewhere, someone else is enduring a similar—or even worse—ordeal.

My hope is that my story will offer encouragement and proof that prayer works, that victory is possible through hope and faith—faith in God's word and in the unseen reality that faith brings. I have experienced the depths of post-traumatic stress disorder, sleepless nights, low moods, depression, anxiety, low self-esteem, and shame. But those are now in my past. They no longer define who I am.

Writing this book is a rare privilege—a legacy for my children and future generations. It is my precious gift to the world, a small offering in hopes that it will touch and help others, even those I may never meet.

Today, I am a survivor. Somebody else is next. As you read, I want you to remember: our stories make us unique, and when we share them, we leave a mark on the lives of others. Human trafficking is real—more real than most can imagine.

I will not overwhelm you with statistics; you can look them up yourself. My aim is to educate, empower, and offer hope. If you are seeking a way out, or know someone who is, let my story be a beacon. If I could escape, you can too.

Names That Define Me
Names carry power. They are more than labels—we inherit them, grow into them, resist them, and eventually embrace them. My names tell the story of who I am, where I come from, and the legacy I carry.

My full name is Unoego Nwaogalanyi Egodi Chinasa Roseline Oiwoh. Roseline is my English name, given to me at baptism. Over the years, people have called me Rose or Rosie, and you may call me Rosie for short.

As a child, I never liked my baptismal names. "Roseline" felt ancient, uncommon, and strange. I often wondered why my godparent chose it. But as I matured, I became curious about my names, their origins, and their meanings. Through inquiry and reflection, I grew to love my name. Today, I introduce myself with pride: I am Roseline, or Rosie. My close friends prefer Rosemary, but each name is a part of me.

My native names—Unoego, Nwaogalanyi, Egodi, Chinasa—carry even deeper meaning.

Unoego, meaning "house of money," is the name my parents gave me. It is the name they've called me since the moment I was born. My father called me Unoego until his last breath. In my village, igbo names are cherished—woven into the very fabric of our identity. They are not just words, but memories, blessings, stories, and prayers.

Egodi, meaning "there is money," is a special name given to me by my maternal grandmother at birth. In our culture, grandmothers often give their grandchildren unique names inspired by the circumstances of their birth. It is an honour, a living memory of the sacred bond between grandmother and grandchild. My mother has continued this tradition, giving each of my children names dear to her heart.

As if that wasn't enough, my maternal aunties and uncles named me Nwaogalanyi, meaning "Child of a wealthy man."

Chinasa means "God answers." In my mother's tongue, "chi" means God, and "nasa" means - answers. It is a daily reminder of our faith and the hope that surrounded my birth.

He lived a full life and passed away in 2018, aged 110. My father was known far and wide as "Nna Unoego"—Unoego's father—a name that became a badge of pride and joy. His legacy lives on.

Adieu, Nna Unoego.
Till we meet again, Papa.
Keep resting, Papa m...

Faith: The Anchor of My Soul

Faith was the foundation of our lives as we grew up. Each day began and ended with prayer. Church wasn't just a ritual — it was our community, our refuge. My mum taught us that faith was more than belief; it was action, hope, and quiet resilience.

In times of hardship, we turned to God, trusting in His provision and mercy. Even as a child, I could feel God's presence — in the rhythm of our days, in the songs we sang, and in the small, grateful moments that filled our home.

That faith became my anchor in the years to come, especially when I faced challenges I could never have imagined — trials that tested my strength, my hope, and my very identity.

Identity: Roots and Wings

My identity is rooted in my family, culture, and faith. Being the first child came with expectations — but also with the privilege of leadership. I learned early the value of hard work, kindness, and hope. My parents, especially my mother, modelled resilience in the face of adversity. Whether tending the farm, cooking meals, or caring for us, she did it all with quiet strength, grace, and unwavering faith.

As I grew older, I became more curious about my names, my heritage, and my place in the world. I began to understand that truly knowing oneself means honouring the stories and sacrifices of those who came before. My names, my family, and my faith are the pillars of my identity. They remind me that I am part of something greater — a lineage of strength, perseverance, and hope.

Seeds of Hope

Looking back, I see how these early experiences laid the foundation for the woman I would become. The stories, songs, and prayers of my childhood became the roots that anchored me, even as life took me far from home.

My journey would lead me through trials I could never have imagined — but the lessons of my beginnings, the power of faith, the strength of family, and the importance of knowing who I am, would carry me through.

This is where my story begins: in a home filled with love, in a land rich with tradition, and in a family bound together by faith. It is a story shaped by the past, but always reaching toward hope.

My Early Passions and Dreams

As a child, I was curious and determined. I loved to learn, to ask questions, and to explore the world around me. My mother especially encouraged my curiosity, teaching me that knowledge was a path to freedom. She would often say, *"My child, a person is limited by what she or he does not know. Seek knowledge."*

I dreamed of becoming educated and working in an office, inspired by the compassion and strength of the women in my family. I wanted to help others, to make a difference, to bring healing and hope.

But I also wanted to change the narrative — to show my family that life has so much more to offer. Life is more than just getting married as soon as a girl's breasts become visible and her menstrual cycle begins, having many children, and working the farm until life ends. These were the patterns I saw, year in and year out. And deep down, I knew: *this couldn't be all there is to life.* Something had to change. When? I didn't know. But I carried that fire in me.

My journey took me to the University of Hertfordshire in the United Kingdom, where I pursued a Bachelor's degree in nursing. The road from my childhood home to becoming a nurse was far more complicated than anyone around me could have imagined. I was trafficked — a reality I kept buried in silence for years. Behind the hope and dreams I carried were chapters filled with fear, confusion, and survival.

I will come back to that part of my story — the part that nearly cut my life short. But for now, I want to begin with the moments that gave me a reason to keep going.

The Joys of Everyday Life

My days are filled with simple joys — prayer, singing, cooking, and spending time with my children. I love to sing, especially when words fail me. Music is how I express myself. It is my way of praising God, lifting my spirit, and finding peace.

Cooking is another passion. I enjoy preparing African delicacies, sharing meals with family and friends, and savouring the flavours and memories of home.

I love to laugh, to watch comedies and documentaries, to meet new people and learn about their cultures. I believe in the power of laughter to heal, to connect, and to bring joy.

"A cheerful heart is good medicine, but a broken spirit saps a person's strength." — Proverbs 17:22

I treasure time with my children — watching them grow, and teaching them the values that shaped me.

Looking Forward

I have many dreams for the future — to further my education, to write more books, and to leave a lasting legacy for my children. I am deeply grateful for the opportunities God has given me — most importantly, the strength to overcome adversity, and the love of family and friends.

As you read my story, I invite you to walk with me through the chapters of my life — to witness not just the struggles, but the faith that sustained me, the family that shaped me, and the identity that carried me forward.

My hope is that my story will inspire you to believe in the power of faith in God's word, the strength of perseverance, and the importance of knowing who you are — your identity.

Chapter 2

Lessons at Home

Home, to me, was never just a building or a place to sleep at night. It was the heartbeat of my earliest memories — the foundation where my character was first shaped. With us, love wasn't always spoken aloud; instead, it was woven into the very fabric of our daily lives — in the food we shared, the chores we helped with, and the rituals that marked our days.

I was the eldest child of my parents, born into a family that later grew to include six siblings, along with half-brothers and half-sisters from my father's other relationships. This made our home lively, sometimes chaotic, but always full of energy and life.

My father, the late Mr. Umadi Odudu — known to all as "Nna Unoego" — was a man of great standing in our village. His name was closely linked to mine; the villagers often called him by my name, a sign of the joy and prosperity my birth was believed to have brought. My mother, on the other hand, was the quiet strength of our household — always busy with her hands but with a heart full of readiness and care.

Growing up in such a family meant I was never alone. There was always someone to talk to, someone to quarrel with, and someone to learn from. But it also came with high expectations. As the first child, I was both the pioneer and the standard — the one most closely watched and often critiqued.

In Igbo culture, the eldest child carries a special burden—a mix of privilege and responsibility. My parents, especially my father, saw more than just a daughter in me; I was a symbol of hope and prosperity. My name, Unoego, means 'house of money,' a reminder of the promise that surrounded my birth. It was a name heavy with expectation.

My father's pride in me was evident in how he introduced me to visitors and how the villagers composed a song in my honour. But along with pride came pressure. I was expected to be a role model for my siblings, excel at school, be respectful and humble, and embody our family's values.

My mother's expectations were just as high, though they came from a different place. She wanted me to be responsible—helping with the endless chores that kept our home running, caring for my younger siblings, and learning the skills that would prepare me to be a good wife and mother someday. She spoke little, but her actions shouted volumes. From dawn until dusk, she was busy cooking, cleaning, washing clothes, fetching water—all while managing to flash a gentle smile or offer a quiet word of encouragement.

Discipline in our home wasn't about punishment alone; it was teaching and guidance. After my parents separated, my mother became the steady hand in our lives. She believed children needed clear boundaries, and she was never afraid to set them. Every part of our day had rules: when to eat, how to treat elders, how to behave at the table, how to dress, and even how to speak.

I remember the sharp sting of her words when I missed a chore or the disappointed frown when my grades slipped. But I also remember the pride shining in her eyes when I succeeded—the quiet joy of knowing I had made her proud.

At times, I resented the strictness and longed for freedom. I envied friends whose parents were more lenient. But now, looking back, I see those lessons as blessings. They taught me the value of hard work, resilience, and strength through adversity.

If discipline was the framework, values were the foundation of our home. My mother instilled in us deep respect for honesty, kindness, and integrity. We were taught to speak the truth no matter how hard, to treat others with respect, to share what we had, and to help those in need.

Faith was another cornerstone. My mother's unshakeable belief in God was woven into daily prayers and visits to orphanages. She reminded us every day that all we had—our farm, our home, our health, our happiness—were gifts from God, and we should be grateful.

These values weren't just words; they were lived in every moment. They showed in how we treated cousins, neighbours, aunties, and uncles, in the meals we shared, and in the care we had for each other. This unseen heritage is my mother's legacy to me—a tradition I carry with pride.

As a child, I craved my parents' approval above all. I wanted to be the good daughter, the good sister, the good person. Their approval shaped many of my choices, pushing me to work harder, seek perfection, and avoid failure.

Sometimes, this desire felt overwhelming. I feared disappointing my mother, measuring my worth by her smile, her nod, or the rare words of praise.

But over time, I realised her approval was love in disguise. Even when strict, her expectations were born from care and hope. She believed in me, and her approval was her way of showing it.

Some of my fondest memories revolve around our family table. Food was more than nourishment—it was celebration and connection. My mother could transform simple ingredients into meals full of flavour and love, weaving comfort and tradition into every bite.

On market day, the sun had barely climbed above the tall palm trees when the first voices began to call out along the red-earth road — *Orie! Orie! Taa bu Orie!* (Today is Orie!). In our village, Orie was more than just a market day; it was the heartbeat of the community.

The air was thick with the sweet and spicy scent of freshly harvested yams, ripe plantains, and sizzling street food. The warm earth beneath my feet seemed to hum with energy as women tied their *ichafu* (head scarves) firmly over their hair, balancing woven baskets brimming with bright oranges, green peppers, and handwoven crafts. Their laughter bubbled like a clear stream as they exchanged stories and greetings, weaving a rich tapestry of sound and life.

When my mother took me along, I felt a mix of excitement and wonder. The colours dazzled me — scarlet chillies hanging in bunches, golden corn drying in the sun, and the deep purples of eggplants gleaming under the morning light. I reached out to touch the smooth skin of a mango, its sweetness almost tangible in the humid air.

I heard the rhythmic tapping of a wooden mortar and pestle nearby, and the chatter of vendors bargaining loudly, their voices rising and falling like music. Occasionally, a distant drumbeat would roll in from the village square, calling everyone to pause and remember the traditions that bound us.

Meanwhile, my siblings stayed behind, cared for by my maternal aunts, their soft laughter fading into the background as my mother and I stepped further into the vibrant crowd. In those moments, surrounded by life's simple pleasures, I felt connected — to my family, my village, and the stories that shaped us.

Going to the market was my favourite thing as a child. The air near the market carried a hundred scents — the sharp tang of freshly ground pepper, the sweetness of ripe pawpaw, the warm comfort of roasted plantain, and the earthy aroma of freshly cooked Okpa (Bambara nut) simmering in palm oil, perfectly wrapped in glossy plantain leaves.

Traders called out their prices in singsong voices, each trying to outdo the other, while children darted between stalls, clutching a few coins to spend on groundnuts or slices of sweet coconut. We moved from one seller to another, carefully selecting foodstuffs my mother believed would be enough until the next market day. The bleats of goats mingled with the clanging of tin bowls as fishmongers displayed their fresh catch from the nearby river. A butcher's machete thudded rhythmically against his wooden chopping block. Nearby, under a wide umbrella, an elderly woman sold herbs and roots, her deeply lined face holding the stories of many lifetimes.

Sweet mother, how can I ever forget the way she moved through the market with purpose and care? From one cloth seller to another, she would carefully run her fingers over the fabrics, feeling their texture as if searching for a secret promise. Her eyes narrowed slightly as she priced panties, dresses, and slippers — every purchase weighed with the hopes of making us comfortable and proud.

She didn't rush. Every item was chosen with love, a silent prayer whispered with each step. I remember how her face softened when she found the right dress — a small victory amidst the everyday struggles. And though the market was loud and bustling, her patience never wavered.

Watching her, I learned what it meant to carry a family's dreams on your shoulders, to fight quietly and fiercely for those you love. It was in those moments, walking beside her, that I first understood the depth of her sacrifices, the tenderness beneath her strength.

Orie was not just about buying and selling — it was where news spread faster than the harmattan wind. It was where promises were made, disputes were settled, and eyes met shyly over baskets of tomatoes. By midday, the market hummed like a beehive, and the whole village seemed to sway to its rhythm.

On our return from the market, the comforting aroma of my mother's cooking would fill the air. She prepared special meals — thick, rich egusi soup bubbling with tender stockfish and smoky dried catfish, roasted pork with crispy edges, all garnished with fresh, vibrant ugwu leaves. The freshly pounded akpu (fufu) was soft and smooth, perfect for dipping and savouring every bite. We gathered around one plate, our hands reaching in eagerly, sharing not just food but laughter, stories, and the warmth of togetherness. Each mouthful seemed to stitch us closer together, weaving invisible threads of love and belonging.

Fish was never scarce in our home, thanks to my father, a hardworking farmer and skilled fisherman. The fresh and dried fish we sold at the market helped provide the little extras — sugar, salt, kerosene — essentials that kept our household running smoothly. But these meals were never just about the food. They were moments of connection, a sanctuary of security in a sometimes uncertain world. Through those shared plates, I learned the true meaning of family — that even in the smallest gestures, there is strength, hope, and unspoken love.

Yet, life wasn't always so gentle. I can still feel the pounding of my heart, the sharp sting of fear when a stray dog suddenly charged at me in my uncle's compound upon my first arrival in Onitsha. The panic, the desperate sprint, and the pounding adrenaline left a lasting imprint on my young mind — a stark lesson in vulnerability and the unpredictability of life. It was a reminder that no matter how sheltered you think you are, the world can surprise you with challenges you never expected.

Being the first daughter – *Ada*, in an Igbo household meant that there were things expected of me, things I was supposed to learn, and habits I was supposed to develop. It's an honour with great responsibilities in Igbo culture. It's not just about birth order; it's about role, identity, and the way the community sees you. She carries the pride of the family name and is expected to lead by example in behaviour, respect, and hard work. For many, being the *Ada* is a badge of pride. It means having a voice in family matters, being trusted with secrets, and being remembered in proverbs like: *Ada bụ isi ụlọ*. (The first daughter is the head of the household).

My mother worked hard to instruct me in the ways of cooking, cleaning, doing the work of younger siblings, and standing tall with dignity and poise. She also taught me to be tough, to be resilient, and to stand up for myself and others.

She was a working model of hard work and determination, demonstrating to me that a woman could be nurturing and powerful, gentle and strong.

My father, also, had things to teach me about what it was to be a daughter, a sister, a future wife and mother. He wanted me to be respectful, to bring honour to our family name, to keep our traditions. But he also taught me to seek my education, to dream big, and to think that I could do anything I wanted to do.

With so many brothers and sisters, our household was never quiet. There were disputes and competitions, jealousy and rivalries. But there was also laughter, companionship, and a profound sense of loyalty. We learned to share, to compromise, to stand by each other in times of trouble and of joy.

Being the eldest, I had to play many roles in my family: the mediator, helper, and occasional substitute parent. I assisted with my siblings' studies, resolved conflicts, and attempted to be a good role model. I learned leadership, responsibility, and empathy from these experiences.

Not all of the lessons were explicitly taught. Some were learned indirectly, by observing the manner in which my mother interacted with others, with us, and with the world at large. I witnessed the sacrifices they made, the way they kept our needs before their own, the unspoken strength that kept them going when things got tough.

I discovered that love is not always dramatic or loud; sometimes it is in the little things, the gentle touch, the quiet encouragement. I discovered that family is not always just about blood, but about commitment, about standing by each other no matter what.

The home lessons I received have remained with me all my life. They have moulded my personality, influenced my decisions, and provided me with the courage to overcome obstacles. They have instilled in me the value of discipline, the significance of values, and the strength of love and approval.

Looking back at childhood, I realised that my mother provided me with a solid foundation. She did her best not to get me married early like other first Daughters I know. In my village, once a girl starts growing breasts and menstruating, she is considered ready for marriage. She listened to my desire to be a graduate someday, even though we were very poor. She was the expectations that challenged me to be better; she was the discipline that taught me perseverance; she was the values that instilled in me moral fibre; and she was the approval that gave me the confidence booster to chase dreams.

Home was never simple, but it was always a home of expansion, of education, of love. I learned there are the seeds from which I still grow, the anchor that holds me down, and the light that shines ahead.

Chapter 3

First Responsibilities

Stepping Into Responsibility

Being the firstborn in a rural Igbo family in Anambra State, Nigeria, responsibility wasn't something I could choose—it was a way of life. From an early age, I was expected to help around the house, care for my siblings, and support the family on the farm. It was both a privilege and a burden—one I learned to carry with quiet pride, even during moments when it felt too heavy to bear.

My earliest memories of responsibility are stitched into the fabric of our daily routines. As soon as I could walk steadily and understand simple instructions, my mother began giving me small tasks. At first, they were simple: drawing water from the clay pot in the kitchen, sweeping the red dust from our compound, or gathering scattered clothes for washing. But as I grew older, those tasks grew with me—and so did the expectations.

As the oldest, I was often my mother's right hand. I helped her care for my younger siblings—making sure they were fed, bathed, and kept safe. Sometimes, this meant waking up before dawn to help prepare breakfast—usually a steaming pot of pap or slices of yam, served with a little palm oil or leftover stew from the night before. I remember standing over the fire, stirring slowly as the morning light crept in. My mother would glance over and give a small, approving nod. That nod spoke volumes: *"You're doing well, my daughter."*

The Rural Environment: Life in Anambra State

Our village was a mosaic of mud-brick houses, each with its own little compound. There was always the familiar buzz of life — roosters crowing, goats bleating, and women exchanging warm greetings as they walked past. During the rainy season, the land turned green and lush, with cassava, yam, and maize growing in well-tended rows. In the dry season, the soil would harden and crack, and dust rose into the air, clinging to everything in its path.

Our house was modest but full of love and life. My mother was a whirlwind — always on the move, always doing something. She rose at dawn, her wrapper tightly cinched at the waist, ready to begin the day's work. I would trail behind her, eager to learn and help. My siblings and I swept the compound with long brooms cut from palm leaves, laughing as we raced to see who could finish first.

Water was precious. We fetched it from different village streams, balancing heavy buckets on our heads. The journey was long, but it was filled with songs, laughter, and stories. My mother would share tales about our people — stories of strong women and wise men — and I would listen with pride swelling in my chest. These stories, told with love and reverence, were lessons in strength, humility, and identity.

I still remember the games and traditions that filled our days. My grandmother's storytelling (akụkọ ifo) brought to life the mischievous tortoise and his clever, sometimes greedy, escapades — each one ending with a moral we were expected to learn. We played *Okwe* (board games), *Suwe* (hopscotch), and *Ten-Ten* with cousins and neighbours, our laughter ringing across the compound.

There were festivals too — the *Masquerade* (*Mmanwu*) dances, the *New Yam* (*Iri Ji*) celebrations, and the Coconut (*Akuoba/Akuoyibo*) festivities. We sang, danced, and beat drums late into the night at *moonlight tales* gatherings, our joy echoing under the stars.

And then there were the proverbs — the treasured wisdom of the elders. My grandmother had a saying for every situation. Her *ilu Igbo* (Igbo proverbs) were short, sharp teachings wrapped in metaphor and meaning. They shaped our behaviour, corrected our missteps, and reminded us of who we were.

- *"Anagwa ntị ma ntị anụghị, ebere isi ntị esoro ya."*
  Translation: "You can tell the ear, but if the ear does not hear, compassion causes the head to follow it."
  Meaning: If you don't listen to advice, consequences will surely follow.
- *"Egbe bere, ugo bere, nke si ibe ya ebena, nku kwaa ya."*
  Translation: "Let the kite perch, let the eagle perch; if one denies the other, may its wings break."
  Meaning: Live and let live. Strength and harmony come from coexistence, not competition.
- *"Onye buru chi ya ụzọ, ọ gbagbue onwe ya n' ọsọ."*
  Translation: "He who runs ahead of his destiny may stumble."
  Meaning: Don't rush your path. Resilience comes from patience and pacing.

These beautiful memories — the stories, the songs, the discipline, the joy — remain with me. They continue to guide me, reminding me of where I come from and who I am. They are the foundation of everything I've become.

Daily Routines and the Weight of Duty

Every day in our village was as routine as the drumbeat. Mornings were for work-sweeping, fetching water, washing clothes, and assisting with food preparation. After breakfast, my siblings and I would trudge down the long, dusty road to school, our feet sending clouds flying as we trudged. The walk was almost two miles in each direction, but we never even considered it. It was just life. We were used to it.

At market days, the village was filled with colours and noise. My mother would take me with her to assist in carrying baskets of goods-yams, cassava, rice, okra, vegetables, and occasionally palm oil or dried fish. From an early age, I learned how to haggle with the market women, how to identify the greenest vegetables, and how to watch out for my younger siblings amidst the crowded stalls.

Afternoons were spent on more work and, if there was time, some more play. My brothers and sisters and I would run around the compound, laughing; the sound of our play blended with the rest of the village sounds. But being the oldest, I always had an awareness of what was expected of me. If a brother or sister fell and bruised a knee, I had to take care of them. If my mother required assistance in the kitchen, I was there, learning how to pound yams, cassava or stir a foaming pot of egusi or ogbono (draw) soup.

Evenings were spent together. My mother would prepare a large pot of soup, and we would all share from the same plate, sitting on mats in the evening light. After supper, my siblings and I would assist with washing the dishes and cleaning up before coming together for family prayers. My mother's voice would ring out in song, and I would sing along, feeling the comfort of family and faith.

Lessons in Endurance and Leadership
Responsibility was never simple. There were times when I wished I could run wild, play carefree and unencumbered. But I knew, even then, that my position mattered. My parents relied on me, and my younger siblings admired me.

I learned to be patient, to prioritise others' needs over mine, and to labour even when I was weary.

There were instances when the responsibility was a heavy burden. I recall during one rainy season that my mother became ill. Farming could not be postponed, so I took over, assisting my father in the fields and looking after my siblings at home. It was tiring, but I was proud to be able to support my family during a challenging moment.

These experiences moulded me, exposing me to endurance and resilience. I understood that true leadership is not ordering people around, but leading them for their benefits. It is being reliable, empathetic, and powerful-even if you are weak.

The First Major Task: Caring for My Siblings

In my opinion, perhaps the greatest burden I was entrusted with — and the first real responsibility of my young life — was the care of my siblings. As the oldest child, it fell on me to look after them whenever our mother was away at the farm or attending to other obligations in the village.

It was no easy task.

My younger siblings were adventurous and endlessly curious, always finding new ways to get themselves into trouble. It was my job to protect them, to teach them right from wrong, and to comfort them when they were frightened or hurt.

I had to learn patience — how to listen, how to speak gently, how to guide without scolding. Sometimes that meant breaking up arguments over toys or the last piece of roasted yam. Other times, it meant helping with homework, or passing down songs and stories my mother had learned from her own mother.

In caring for my siblings, I came to understand the deeper meaning of kindness, compassion, and responsibility. It wasn't just about watching over them — it was about helping them grow, even while I was still growing myself.

The Spiritual Side of Responsibility

Faith was woven into every part of our daily lives. My parents made sure we went to church every Sunday, no matter how tired we were or how far the walk. Church wasn't just about religion — it was about discipline, structure, and community. It gave us a place to belong and a path to follow.

Sundays always stood apart from other days. The village would slow down. Mothers usually stayed home from their daily work, and even the air seemed quieter, more respectful. I liked that we rested more on Sundays. It was seen as a holy day, a day to be still and turn our hearts toward God.

Our local Catholic church had whitewashed walls and wooden pews that creaked beneath our weight. The Reverend Father, dressed in his flowing robes, would speak of Jesus Christ with such certainty that I couldn't help but listen closely. I didn't always understand everything he said, but something about his voice — deep, calm, and powerful — stirred something in me.

I remember one Sunday in particular. I must have been about six or seven years old. The Reverend spoke about heaven — not just as a place far away, but as something we could begin to live for here and now. He said, "To walk in love is to walk toward heaven."

That line stayed with me.

As I sat in the wooden pew beside my siblings, their legs swinging restlessly, I remember feeling a strange quiet settle over me. It was the first time I felt the weight of spiritual responsibility — the sense that being a good daughter, a good sister, and a good person wasn't just about following rules. It was about aligning my life with something sacred.

And then came the part of the Mass that always moved me the most: when the Reverend began to pray in Latin.

"Dominus vobiscum."
The Lord be with you.
And the congregation would respond, almost in unison:
"Et cum spiritu tuo."
And with your spirit.

Even though we were children, we knew what to say. The Latin had become familiar to us — a language we didn't speak in everyday life but somehow understood in church. We had heard it so many times, we could almost anticipate the rhythm of the prayers. And when the Reverend ended with a solemn phrase like *"In nomine Patris, et Filii, et Spiritus Sancti"* — *In the name of the Father, and of the Son, and of the Holy Spirit* — we would all respond without hesitation:

"Amen."

The language rolled over us like a gentle wave — ancient, mysterious, and full of power. I didn't understand all the words, but I understood the feeling. A stillness would fill the room. Eyes would close. Some women would clutch their rosaries tighter. In those moments, it felt like something holy had entered the space — something too big to explain, yet so present you could almost touch it.

I felt small, but not afraid. I felt part of something eternal.

Even at home, spirituality was never limited to the church. My grandmother would often sit under the mango tree in the late afternoon, rosary in hand, whispering prayers — and then turn around and quote a proverb that held just as much spiritual truth. She believed in the power of both Christian faith and Igbo wisdom. For her, they were not separate paths, but one wide road to truth.

"Nwata kịrị nkọ, ya hụ chi ya kụọ ya aka," she once told me. *A child who washes their hands will dine with elders. Meaning*: If you live responsibly and respectfully, even the heavens will recognize you.

In our world, to be responsible wasn't just to carry out chores or care for siblings — it was to live in a way that honored God, family, and tradition. Responsibility was spiritual. It was moral. And it was expected of me, even as a child.

I carried that sense with me — through every task, every prayer, every time I helped my siblings or listened to my mother's quiet instructions. And even now, when life feels overwhelming, I remember that holy silence on a Sunday morning... the echo of Latin prayers under the high ceiling... and the soft but sure voice of the congregation, all of us — young and old — saying, Amen.

I recall being puzzled by some of the church teachings — especially the instruction not to read the Bible on our own. It confused me. Why wouldn't we be encouraged to seek God personally? Even as a child, I felt a deep desire to know Him for myself — not just through the voice of the Reverend Father, but in my own heart.

That longing only grew stronger after a vision I had at a very young age — a moment I can still recall with clarity. I cannot explain it fully, but it left me more inclined to spiritual things. I began to pay attention — not just to prayers and church sermons, but to quiet moments, dreams, and the gentle stirrings in my spirit. I wanted to understand my purpose. I wanted to live a life that honoured God.

At the same time, I carried another desire in my young heart: I wanted to become a graduate. That word, *graduate*, sounded like hope to me. It felt like something that could change everything — for me, for my family, for the future I couldn't yet see. Even when doors were closed and obstacles seemed too great, I believed in what others called impossible.

Prayer and quiet reflection began to teach me that responsibility was more than completing chores or watching over my siblings. True responsibility meant being honest with myself, faithful in small things, and open to God's voice. It meant loving others — not just in words, but through sacrifice, forgiveness, and service. It meant asking, again and again, *"Lord, what would You have me do?"*

Responsibility, I learned, was spiritual. It was the quiet choice to trust, to obey, and to dream — even when no one else believed.

The Beauty and Challenge of Rural Life

But faith was not just something we felt in church or in quiet prayer. It was lived every day, in the soil beneath our feet and the rhythm of the seasons that shaped our lives. Life in Anambra State was both beautiful and difficult.

The soil was fertile and rich, promising harvests, but farming was backbreaking work under an often unforgiving sky. The wet season brought heavy rains that nourished the land but sometimes washed away the hard-won crops. The dry season baked the earth until it cracked, and the sun bore down mercilessly.

There were days we walked to school barefoot, the hot sun burning our feet and skin. There were times when hunger gnawed at our bellies, and moments when sickness or troubles threatened to overwhelm us. Yet, despite these challenges, life here held a deep, quiet beauty — in the laughter of children, the rhythm of the seasons, and the steady pulse of community.

But there was also a strong sense of community. Neighbours helped one another in times of need, freely giving and receiving food, labour, and support. Market days became celebrations, filled with music, laughter, and stories that echoed through the village. Family gatherings were brightened by shared joy and the comfort of togetherness.

Looking back, I appreciate those times deeply. They taught me the value of hard work, the importance of family, and above all, the resilience that faith and community can inspire — even in the face of life's greatest challenges.

Looking Back: The Foundation for the Future

My early duties as a child laid the foundation for everything that followed. They taught me to be strong, to endure, and to lead with kindness. From those simple beginnings, I gained the courage to face challenges, the wisdom to guide others, and the faith to keep going — even when the road was hard.

As I grew older and stepped into new roles — student, nurse, wife, mother — I carried those early lessons with me. The skills I learned in the village, the values passed down from my mother and grandmother, and the faith that sustained me through adversity have all shaped the person I've become.

I am especially grateful to my parents — and to my mother, most of all — for trusting me, for giving me opportunities to serve and lead, and for teaching me through example. The lessons I learned on the red earth and green pastures of Anambra State were never easy, but they were a gift — a gift that has carried me through every season of life.

Chapter 4

The Journey That Chose Me

Dear Reader,
These early responsibilities were never easy, yet they were a gift — one that unknowingly prepared me for the journeys ahead and, incredibly, carried me through every season of life.

But not all beginnings felt like a gift at the time.
Some came wrapped in confusion and silence — moments I wouldn't fully understand until years later.

One of those moments began with a small black bag.

The Black Bag

The night my mother packed a small black bag for me, I thought I was going to school. I didn't know I was walking into my first job as a housemaid.

I was seven years old, wide-eyed with hope. For months, my mother had promised that in January, I would finally start school. I dreamed of wearing a uniform, carrying exercise books, and joining my cousins in class. I imagined writing my name on a slate, speaking English like the children in the city. It was the kind of dream that kept me alive in a village where we wore *Okirika* (second-hand) clothes, torn and faded, passed from one child to another until the fabric gave way.

But my mother had only 50 naira left after Christmas. I remember the heaviness in her voice as she whispered to me that she could not afford school fees, a bag, or even shoes. She tried to sound strong, but her tears betrayed her. That night, she explained my uncle and his wife, Caro had already spoken. They agreed I would go with them to the city. My mother believed it was for the best.

She held me tightly, her arms trembling around me. *"Be obedient,"* she said. *"Be teachable. Listen to your Madam. It will be well with you."*

I didn't argue. I didn't refuse. I was too young to question, too trusting to suspect. My heart ached to leave my siblings and her, but I carried my black bag and walked toward what I believed was a brighter future.

My first time in the city

When we arrived in Onitsha, I was dazzled. My uncle's house seemed like another world. His children wore neat clothes that smelled of soap and perfume. They spoke English with an ease that made me feel invisible. My uncle, fresh and confident, barely noticed me. But the housemaid, Esther, did.

Esther became my shield. She took me on errands, taught me how to take a bath, speak simple English words, and even bought me medicine when I became sick from a fever and rashes. Esther made me understand it was a change of environment. When others mocked me, she defended me. In her care, I felt seen.

Then, one evening, everything changed.

Caro introduced me to a woman named Tessa. She smiled as though she was offering me a gift, but her words pierced me instead: *"Rose, this is my friend. You will live with her. She will start school for you. Be a good girl."*

I turned to my uncle, waiting for him to explain. He said nothing. Not a word.

Tears blurred my eyes as I fetched my little black bag once more. Esther hugged me, wiping my cheeks with her hands, whispering, *"Don't cry. Everything will be alright."* But when I left that house, following a stranger, I knew something had been stolen from me. My childhood was no longer mine.

Life with Aunty Tessa was not what I expected—and yet, in some ways, it was more. She was strict but kind. She woke me at 4 a.m. for prayers, taught me discipline in her shop, and trusted me with money and goods. Unlike many maids, I was never sent to hawk on the streets. She bought me clothes, new underwear in dozens, and spoke words that lit a fire inside me:

"Rose, if you remain this honest and obedient, I will train you up to university level."

For the first time, I felt valued.

I will never forget the day she took me back to my mother, carrying over 5 big yams, big bag of rice, Ankara wrappers, and money. My mother danced with joy, calling the neighbours to come and see. Her eyes glistened with pride, and for once, I felt like the child she always dreamed I'd become.

But that visit cost me more than I could have imagined.

When Caro heard, she was furious. She stormed into our shop one afternoon, pacing the floor, her voice sharp and cutting. *"Don't call me your friend!"* she snapped at Tessa, jabbing her finger in the air. I watched in silence, my chest pounding, as the woman who had once promised to help me now turned into my captor.

Weeks later, the final blow came. On a visit to my uncle's house, I was ordered to stay behind. I watched through tear-filled eyes as Tessa pleaded, even kneeling on the floor, begging them to let me return with her. Caro refused. My uncle sat in silence—his silence louder than any words.

By the next morning, my black bag was back in their house.

That was how my first job as a housemaid ended.

I was only eight years old, but I had already learned what betrayal sounded like: silence.

Chapter 5

A Life of Silence

Amanda's House

Caro and my Uncle didn't return me to my mother. Instead, she handed me over again—this time to a woman called Amanda.

Amanda's house stood tall on a hill, painted bright, with iron gates that seemed to swallow me the moment I stepped through them. She was a nurse—proud and commanding—with a sharp voice and eyes that missed nothing. Her husband was rarely around, so Amanda ruled the house alone. From the first day, I knew: I was not a child in her care. I was her servant, despite having four children – three were older, and her last child was the same age as me. They were two boys and two girls.

A Life of Chores

Before the sun even thought about rising, I was already awake, my body moving in a rhythm it had known for years. The room was still dark and silent except for the scraping of my hands against the floor and the clinking of plates as I washed them again and again. My fingers felt raw, my back ached, but I kept going because if I slowed down, Amanda's voice would cut through the stillness like a whip.

"You're too slow, Rose! Hurry up! If you want to go to school, you must finish quickly—my day depends on it!"

Her own children had eaten breakfast and gone to school on time. Meanwhile, I moved quietly—like I didn't exist. I would cry silently, most times within me, burying the tears so she wouldn't see. I didn't want her to notice. If she did, I risked being beaten—or worse, told not to go to school at all.

Out of five school days in a week, I was late for most. Some days, I didn't go at all. Instead, by mid-morning, I was already walking through the busy streets of Onitsha, hawking puff-puff under the weight of the sun.

On my head was a big, transparent rectangular box, packed full and sealed shut. In one hand, I carried a black waterproof bag stuffed with extra buns and puff-puff for refills.

Dust clung to my skin, eyes, and nose. Sweat soaked my dress. Shame burned hotter than the afternoon sun as strangers looked at me like I was less than human.

Some mornings, Amanda would call out before I could finish the chores.

"Rose, hurry up and come to the shop! Don't forget, you still have to go to the Onitsha Main Market to buy soup ingredients before school!"

The market was always full—shoulders bumping, traders shouting, queues twisting like snakes between stalls. I asked if I could go later in the day when the crowd would thin. She refused, every time.

So I walked. Twenty-five minutes each way. Sometimes more. I was already exhausted before I even entered the market, and by the time I returned—arms heavy, face dusty, feet sore—it would be past nine in the morning. Amanda would still send me on more errands. And all I could do was obey.

When I cried, it was in silence. I had no one to tell. No one would listen. Amanda didn't care whether I made it to school or not. She didn't ask. She never even looked.

Still, I endured—because I wanted to learn. Because learning felt like my only way out.

After school, there was no rest. I'd take the big transparent box again, balanced it on my head, and hawked through the loud, crowded streets of Mgbuka, Nkpor. My legs trembled, my neck strained, and the sun beat down until I thought I would fall.

Hawking was more than tiring—it was dangerous. Cars sped past carelessly. Sometimes, I had to run across roads, the box swaying dangerously on my head as horns screamed behind me. I was nearly hit once by a motorcycle, and the rider yelled like I was the one who did wrong.

Strange men would call out to me, pretending to buy, asking too many questions. A few tried to touch. I learned to walk quickly, eyes down, heart racing.

Some days, the rain poured while I was still far from home. I had no umbrella. I'd crouch under a stall, soaked to the skin, while water dripped from the puff-puff box. Other times, the sun was so hot I could barely see straight, my slippers melting against the burning pavement.

Once, someone stole buns from my box while I wasn't looking. Amanda didn't believe me. She had already counted the full cost of everything I carried, and when I came back short, I was scolded like a thief.

Before I left to hawk, I sometimes ate a quick lunch—that would be my only real meal until I returned around 7 p.m. or later. Other times, Amanda would give me just one bun to eat. On rare days, I would eat one from the box during hawking. When I told her, she wouldn't always be happy. She had counted every piece, and when I returned, I was expected to give a full account.

She would count the remaining puff-puff and buns one by one, checking my math against hers. No room for mistakes. No understanding. Just the numbers—and the weight of responsibility on a child's shoulders.

Sometimes, I looked at the other children—clean, carefree, walking beside their mothers, eating snacks I could never afford. I wondered what it felt like to be one of them. To be wanted. To be protected. **But one encounter haunts me more than all the others.**

It was during a hot afternoon, around lunchtime. I was walking along a street I knew well when a group of men waved me over. They were inside an uncompleted building—the kind with no windows or doors, just cement blocks, dust, and shadows. One of them called out, asking to buy puff-puff.

Because I wanted to sell, I entered. I thought it would be on the first floor, but when I got there, they told me to come up. "It's upstairs," one of them said. I hesitated. But again—because I wanted to sell—I climbed. Second floor. Third. Fourth. Fifth.

There were about four or five of them sitting around, joking, eating. Something in me felt off, but I didn't listen. I stood there quietly and opened my box.

Then, one of them walked into another room and called me to follow him. "Come collect your money," he said.

I paused. Something in his voice made my stomach twist.

"I will collect the money here," I replied firmly, still standing in the open.

But he refused. "Come here," he insisted, his voice colder now.

I told him again to pay me where I stood. He didn't move. I turned to the others, hoping they would help.

"Tell him to pay me here," I said.

They didn't.

Instead, they started laughing.

I knew what that laugh meant.

And I knew I had to leave.

I picked up my box, my hands shaking, and walked quickly away. My legs felt like jelly as I made my way back down those stairs. My heart was pounding so loudly I couldn't hear anything else. I didn't stop until I reached the road.

That day, I understood something even deeper than hunger or tiredness. I was a child, carrying food and fear around the streets, and I had no protection. Not from the sun. Not from the strangers. Not even from the people I lived with.

When I got home, I told Amanda everything that had happened.

I explained how they called me into the building, how I climbed because I wanted to sell, how the man asked me to follow him into a room alone—and how I refused.

I told her I was scared.

I hoped she would understand. That for once, she would see I wasn't just a seller, a child who cooked and cleaned and counted buns. I hoped she would tell me I did the right thing.

But Amanda didn't say much.

No hug. No "well done." No warning not to go again.

Just silence.

And then, like always, the day moved on.

That was my life.

A life of chores.

A life of silence.

A life I did not choose—but one I survived.

School Wasn't a Refuge. School should have been my escape. But even there, I was reminded of my place.

Amanda's daughter, Akam, walked into class in spotless uniforms, her shoes shining, her hair tied with ribbons. I followed behind, carrying her bag. My own clothes were worn thin. My sandals flapped on the ground. During break, my classmates opened lunchboxes filled with biscuits and meat pies. I had nothing. I drank water and pretended it was enough.

I envied them—their food, their clothes, their laughter. And I hated myself for that envy.

A False Promise

Still, I held onto hope. Amanda once said, "If you work hard, I'll make sure you succeed."

I believed her. After my chores, I studied late into the night, my eyelids heavy, my stomach growling, my hands trembling over the pages. When I brought home good results, she barely glanced at them.

"Okay," she said, without a smile or praise.

That indifference cut deeper than any insult. I served her for over 3 years.

But there were deeper wounds than being overlooked. Some things went beyond broken promises or indifference. One night, something happened that changed how I saw that house — and how I saw myself.

The Torchlight

It was a Friday night. Amanda's children had gone to the monthly church vigil — all except the first son. Amanda and I stayed back. I had returned late from hawking that day, so she asked me to make her dinner and serve it before bed.

By the time I finished cooking and cleaning, it was nearly 11:30 p.m. I rushed to the bathroom, took a quick shower, changed into my nightie, and lay down on the mat on the floor to rest.

Not long after, I felt a hand on me.

I opened my eyes to a harsh beam of light — Amanda's first son was standing over me, shining a torch in my face.

Startled, I sat up and moved to leave the room.

"Be silent," he said.

I refused.

I knew the kind of person he was — he smoked weed, got into fights, and was known for sleeping around. I imagined the worst. My heart was pounding.

Terrified, I ran straight to Amanda's room.

She opened the door, calm and expressionless, as if nothing could possibly be wrong.

"What is it?" she asked.

I told her everything — the torchlight, the touch, the fear that still hadn't left my body.

Without saying a word, she turned and walked to her son's room.

He was lying on his bed, pretending to be asleep.

She looked at him, then at me. Her voice dropped into a whisper, sharp and cold.

"When did this happen, Rose? He's sleeping. Make sure you're not lying about my son."

I stood frozen.

"I hope you're not dreaming," she added. "Go back to the room and sleep. My son is in bed, and you're talking nonsense."

Then she shut her door.

I stood in the hallway, my heart racing, a heavy knot of shame and confusion rising in my throat. I glanced at the big round clock on the living room wall: 3:00 a.m.

The other children still hadn't returned from the vigil.

I couldn't go back into that room. I couldn't sleep. So I sat on the cold corridor floor outside Amanda's door — afraid, exposed, fully awake.

At some point, I heard movement.

Through the window, I saw him.

He was searching for me — checking the toilet, the bathroom, the kitchen, even the living room. Room by room, quietly, patiently.

Then he saw me — sitting by his mother's door.

Our eyes met.

Without a word, he turned and went back to his room.

I didn't move. I didn't blink. I just sat there, frozen, listening to the silence of the house, waiting for the sun.

That was where I stayed — on the cold floor by Amanda's door — until around 5:30 a.m., when the other children finally returned home from church.

He had tried different methods to get to me — all of them failed.

But even in failure, he left damage behind.

That same year, I started my menstrual cycle. My breasts had begun to form. I was just learning about my body, still a child in many ways, yet already carrying fear I didn't have the words for.

I was a virgin. I had never known any man. But Amanda once told me, *"If a man crosses you, you'll become pregnant. If a man even touches you, you'll get pregnant without delay."*

So I lived in fear — not just of being hurt, but of being changed forever by that hurt.

I avoided him at all costs. I hated seeing him. I hated hearing his name. That one night had made everything about him unbearable.

Because he stayed on the university campus most of the time, I began to count the days until holidays would end, praying he would leave again.

His presence was a shadow. And when he was gone, I could finally breathe.

This carried on for a few more months, until Amanda's son finally returned to the university where he was based. His presence lifted a heavy weight from the house, but the fear remained buried deep inside me. My body was free, but my spirit stayed in hiding.

A week after he left, I became very unwell.

Amanda was the first to notice that something wasn't right. I wasn't eating. I had no strength. I was feverish all the time, but at the same time shaking with chills. Sometimes, I would lie down outside in the sun—hoping it would warm the cold that lived inside my bones.

She began to suspect the worst.

"Have you gotten yourself pregnant?" she asked harshly, her voice filled with accusation.

I didn't even have the strength to respond. I was too weak to defend myself.

Amanda called a friend of hers, who was a nurse to check me. But it wasn't pregnancy.

That was when we discovered I had chickenpox, measles, mumps, and rubella—all at once.

My body broke out in itchy, swollen rashes—tiny, angry blisters that burned and stung. They spread quickly—from my face down to my legs. My skin felt like it was on fire. My throat swelled. My joints ached. I couldn't eat, couldn't sleep, couldn't stop scratching even though each touch made it worse. My whole body felt like it had betrayed me.

It was hard to tell where the pain ended and the itching began. My eyes were sensitive to light. My mouth was full of sores. Even swallowing water felt like punishment.

Amanda bought me medication—though I can't remember if it worked or not. The days blurred together in a haze of heat, pain, and darkness.

All I remember is lying there, alone with my thoughts, trying to survive not just the illness, but the life I was living.

Amanda bought me medication—though I can't remember if it worked or not. The days blurred together in a haze of heat, pain, and darkness.

All I remember is lying there, alone with my thoughts, trying to survive not just the illness, but the life I was living.

Even then, Amanda still sent me on errands. My face was swollen, my skin covered in rashes, my body burning with fever—but she didn't stop.

And somehow, I still went.

I knew I was obedient—too obedient, maybe. But what choice did I have? Saying no was never an option. Obedience had become part of me—something stitched into my skin as tightly as the rash that covered it.

This time, I had finished my Common Entrance Examination.
I didn't do well.

And deep down, I wasn't surprised.

How could I have done well, when every morning began with chores and ended in exhaustion? I studied with swollen eyes, heavy limbs, and an empty stomach. My mind was never still enough to focus—only filled with fear, noise, and the pressure to please.

When the results came out, Amanda looked at me and said coldly,

"You have to hawk and raise money to go and collect your result."

It broke something in me.

I had hawked every week for her—Monday to Friday, sometimes Saturdays too. All that effort, and now I had to hawk just to collect the fruit of my own labour. As if my future was something I had to earn permission to touch.

I was just a girl.

A sad girl with no one to talk to.

Since coming to live with Amanda, I had never heard from Caro. Not once. Not from my uncle either. No letter. No phone call. No message. Nothing. When I asked Amanda if she had heard from them, she would always say, "yes, they are fine."

I felt invisible—used and discarded by everyone who was supposed to protect me.

Mobile phones weren't common then. My mother didn't have one. If she did, maybe I would have called… just to hear her voice… to tell her I was still alive.

But I had no voice. No one was listening.

So I did what I always did: I obeyed.

I hawked. I cooked. I cleaned.

And I kept hoping that one day, something would change.

Even when I felt forgotten, I stayed faithful.

I never tasted what it felt like to be in JSS1—Junior Secondary School in Nigeria.

That year, I should have started, just like Amanda's last child did. He wore a new uniform, carried new books, and left the house each morning with hope in his eyes.

Me? I stayed behind, scrubbing floors and hawking puff-puff.

Amanda had the money. That wasn't the problem. She just didn't spend it on me.

And somewhere deep inside, I knew why.

I wasn't her child.

I told myself that over and over again, until it stopped hurting so loudly. Still, it pained me. I knew I deserved more. I had worked hard. I had done everything she asked. I had been obedient—even when it hurt.

But I wasn't one of them. And that reality sat heavy on my chest.

For a while, I mourned it silently. I cried at night when no one could hear. Then, I stopped. Because what could I do?

Eventually, something in me shifted.

Whenever I was alone, I would sit and think—really think—about how far I had come. Despite everything, I had finished primary school. That was something my parents couldn't give me. That was something many girls like me never had the chance to do.

Maybe that was the gift. The only one I'd get.

So I swallowed the pain. I accepted my place. I continued living with Amanda, serving her without pay, without education, without a voice.

Chapter 6

The Day I Was Seen

Before the Queue

But I never stopped hoping.

I continued living with Amanda, moving through her house like a shadow—serving her without pay, without schooling, without even the memory of choice. The days blurred together, like smudged writing on a wall long rained on.

Three of Amanda's children were older than me. They treated me the way their mother did—snapping fingers, calling my name like it was an order, not a person. I was the same age as her youngest, but even he knew the difference between us: he belonged. I did not.

Amanda often took me, her last two children, and a cousin who lived with us to church for prayers—sometimes on Wednesdays, other times on Fridays.

We left early, when the sky was still pale with sleep. Amanda said the queue could be long, especially if you wanted to see the prophetess. We walked to the bus stop in silence, the children half-awake, the roads still yawning open. On the bus, Amanda kept the youngest close, her hand resting on his shoulder, while I stood, or sat only if she allowed it.

She said the prayers were important.

Sometimes they were for guidance—especially when money went missing and no one confessed. The pastor would preach about hidden sins, and Amanda would nod solemnly, as though the Word had confirmed what she already believed. Other times, she stayed long at the altar, whispering her petitions for her first son. I had overheard talk—plans for him to travel abroad, start afresh, rise higher. She prayed for him with something like longing. Almost like love.

She prayed for me too—but never in the same way.

Amanda believed I needed deliverance. Especially me.

She said it plainly, sometimes while folding clothes or stirring a pot, as though it were a fact and not an accusation.

I often wondered what she saw when she looked at me. A problem? A curse? Something she had taken in and now regretted?

But I knew this much:

Whatever Amanda thought lived inside me—whatever evil she hoped to cast out—I was not afraid of it.

What I feared was living like this forever.

And no prayer had ever been said for that.

Later, I overheard her youngest whisper to someone, "Mum went to ask if my brother can travel abroad. She took Rose because I was in school."

The Day I was Seen

At the prayer ground, the process was always the same: You collected a ticket. Sat quietly. Waited to be called.

When our number was finally announced, Amanda and I rose. We entered the room together. The air was thick with silence. Amanda knelt before the prophetess. I sat quietly on the floor beside her, head down, hands in my lap.

Then the prophetess looked at me.

She tilted her head slightly, her eyes narrowing. "Whose child is this?" she asked, pointing at me.

Amanda didn't hesitate.

"She came with me. She is my housemaid."

The woman's eyes didn't leave mine. She studied me like she could see past my skin—into something buried beneath it. Then she spoke—slowly, clearly, her words sinking into the hollows of my chest.

"Hmm..." she said, closing her eyes.

She left Amanda where she was kneeling, and walked toward me.

"You said she is your housemaid?" she repeated, turning to Amanda.
Then, looking back at me, her voice sharpened. "Where is her mother?"

I stayed silent. Not because I didn't know the answer—
But because I had not been given permission to speak.

Amanda glanced at me and nodded.

"She is at my village," I said quietly.

The prophetess stared harder. "Where is your village? What do your parents do?"

"She is a farmer," I replied.

I answered all her questions without looking her in the eyes. In my culture, it is disrespectful to hold the gaze of elders when speaking. I kept my eyes low, even as I studied her without meaning to:

Her skin was light. She wore a brown bubu gown, her hair tied with a scarf. Her sandals were open-toed. The only time I dared to lift my head was when she began pacing—slow, deliberate steps, as though delivering a message from somewhere far away.

It felt like a strange encounter. One I would never forget.

She behaved like a guard—sent on an errand. A guard who must deliver the message by all means necessary.

Then she stopped in front of me.

"Get up from the floor," she said.

I didn't move until Amanda told me to. Only then did I stand.

The prophetess placed both hands on my shoulders. Her voice dropped lower, but her words were clear, like someone reading from a letter that had been sealed long ago.

"I see a bright future ahead of her. She will be great. But there are many thorns along her journey. She will go abroad... but I do not know how. She will be the one her family will look upon for help in years to come."

Amanda thanked her.

She took my hand, and together we left the room, back to the shop.
Back to reality.

But the words followed me.

For a long time, I said nothing. I didn't even fully understand what it meant. But something in me stood taller. Amanda looked at me as we stood up to leave. She didn't say anything, but she held my hand—tightly. Tighter than usual. It was the first time anyone had ever looked at me and seen a future.

As we stepped out of the prophetess's room, the afternoon sun greeted us—hot and sharp, like it didn't care what had just happened inside.

Amanda didn't say a word.

She held my hand tighter than usual. Not lovingly—just firmly, as if afraid to let go of something she didn't quite understand.

I walked beside her in silence, the prophetess's words ringing in my ears, each one like a tiny light flickering inside me.

Her future is bright.

She will go abroad... but I do not know how.

She will be great.

She will be the one to rescue her family.

No one had ever said those kinds of things about me. No one had ever looked at me and seen anything more than a housemaid or a burden.

But she did.

Even if Amanda forgot it the moment, we left... Even if I returned to chores, to hawking, to silence and beatings...
I didn't forget.

I carried those words with me like a secret treasure, hidden where no one could steal it.

That night, as I lay on the mat in the corner of the room, I whispered them to myself like a prayer:

She said I'll be great.

She said I'll go abroad.

She said I'll be the one to rescue my family.

I didn't know how.

I didn't know when.

But for the first time in a long time... I believed.

Chapter 7

The Lie That Changed Everything

The Plan I Didn't See

There was a man from the church we all attended. He was also from my village.

Amanda would greet him warmly whenever he came around, and I noticed he started visiting her more often — sometimes at the shop, other times at the house. Whenever he came, they would speak privately, always behind closed doors, their voices low and serious.

I didn't think much of it at first. He was familiar. He was from home.

He was also a good friend of my uncle's.

One evening, Amanda called me to the front of the shop. The man was standing there beside her.

She introduced him to me properly.

"This is Uncle Dominic," she said. "He's from your village. He knows your mother."

I remember the wave of emotion that ran through me — a strange mix of relief and joy.

For the first time in a long time, I felt a sliver of safety. Someone here in the city knew my mother. Someone here knew me — not as Amanda's housemaid, but as a child from his own village.

Maybe, just maybe, I had someone I could run to. Someone who could speak for me. Protect me. Tell my mother how I was doing.

I didn't know that behind the smiles and soft greetings... They already had a plan.

A plan that had nothing to do with protecting me.

And everything to do with using me.

Accused

A few weeks later, something happened — something I never imagined, not even in my worst dreams.

Amanda's younger sister returned from her NYSC. (NYSC — the National Youth Service Corps — is a one-year mandatory program for Nigerian university graduates. Most people return home with stories, certificates... and in her case, a fiancé.)

She came back glowing, confident, and clearly excited about her new life.
Her fiancé visited often. He was polite and well-dressed. I barely spoke to him beyond a quiet greeting or a respectful nod.

Then, one morning... it started.

A whisper. A sideways glance. A sudden coldness I couldn't explain.

Before I could piece it together, an accusation had been made:

That I had been admiring her fiancé.

That I loved him.

That I had been watching him closely and trying to get his attention.

I was frozen. Shocked. Speechless.

I couldn't even form the words to defend myself — because nothing like that had ever happened.

But it didn't matter. The damage was done.

The way Amanda looked at me changed.

The way her sister spoke around me changed.

The silence in the room whenever I entered told me exactly what they now believed.

Everyone believed the lie.

I cried.

Not just because I was being falsely accused — but because even in my innocence, no one defended me.

No one asked me what happened.

No one asked how I felt.

They just believed the worst.

I cried myself to sleep that night, and many nights after. Tears from a place too deep for words — the kind that burn more from confusion than pain.

All I ever wanted was peace.

But even silence wasn't safe anymore.

Amanda asked me quietly,

"Rose... is it true?"

My heart was pounding. I didn't even know how to respond. I hadn't done anything wrong — but I'd already seen how things were spiralling. I was scared, confused, tired.

So, I answered the only way I could.

"No ma... it's not true."

But Amanda's reaction told me she didn't believe me.

She gave me that look — a mixture of disappointment and accusation, the kind that doesn't need words to crush someone. I stood there, numb, the room shrinking around me.

Later that evening, her husband came home. He didn't ask me anything directly. But I saw it in the way he looked at me — like something had shifted.

He believed it too.

The weight of the house turned heavy with judgment. Their voices, their silences, their eyes — all of it wrapped around me like rope.

Only one person stood up for me.

Amanda's second-to-last child — the quiet one, the one who usually stayed out of adult business — spoke out.

"Mummy, I don't think Rose could do that. She's too innocent. She doesn't even talk to him."

But his voice was small. And in that house, the majority carried the vote.

His words were drowned by the louder silence of others.

No one else defended me.

No one else questioned the lie.

And even though I had spoken the truth, it didn't matter.

Chapter 8

Sent Away Without a Word

The Weight of Lies

After the accusation, life in Amanda's house shifted in a way I never imagined possible.

The days grew colder.

The silence between me and Amanda stretched longer — heavy with unspoken anger and disappointment. Her eyes no longer met mine without suspicion.

Amanda stopped speaking to me kindly. Instead, her words were sharp, clipped, like daggers thrown in passing.

"You think you can just come here and steal from us?" she'd snap when I was near. Even when there was no reason for her anger, I felt it everywhere.

Amanda's husband avoided looking at me altogether. His presence was like a shadow that followed, judging silently.

The other children whispered behind my back, throwing me looks I couldn't read but knew weren't good.

I became invisible and yet the center of a storm I never caused.

The only comfort was the quiet voice of the second-to-last child, who still sometimes gave me a small smile or a kind word.

Punishment came swiftly and without mercy.

If I hesitated or slowed in my chores, I was beaten.

If I asked for water, I was told to work harder.

If I made a mistake, even a small one, Amanda's anger exploded.

I cried myself to sleep many nights, not only from the pain on my skin but the pain inside my heart — the ache of being blamed for something I never did, of being alone in a crowded room.

Yet, through it all, the words of the prophetess lingered somewhere deep inside me — that I would be great, That I would be a light to my family, that I would rescue them.

Those words were now my only shield, my only hope.

And so, I endured.

The Flicker of Hope

Every day was a test of endurance.

But deep inside me, something refused to be broken.

The prophetess's words played on repeat in my mind, like a gentle song guiding me through the darkness:

"Her future is bright...

She will be a light to her family...She will be great."

I clung to those words like a lifeline.

When Amanda's harsh voice filled the house, I reminded myself that this was not the end of my story.

When my hands were raw from scrubbing floors and my feet ached from endless hawking, I whispered to myself, *"One day, this will change."*

Sometimes, when I was alone, I allowed myself to dream. Dream of a life beyond the cramped rooms, beyond the harsh words, beyond the weight of suspicion.

I imagined a place where I could study without fear. Where I could laugh without worry. Where I could be more than a servant, more than a shadow.

I held onto that vision with all my heart.

It was the small flicker inside me — quiet but unyielding — that kept me going.

No matter how dark the nights, no matter how heavy the days,
I would not let go of hope.

Because I knew deep down, I was meant for more.

December 2006 was the last time I hawked.

Come January 2007 — first week — the streets slowly came alive again.

By the second week, most traders were back. Shops reopened. Streets filled with voices, music, and movement.

But Amanda said nothing about our shop.

She didn't mention reopening.

No instructions. No plans.

Instead, she became... kind.

Softer in her tone.

Gentler in her corrections.

A small part of me lit up with hope.

Maybe she's had a change of heart, I thought. *Maybe she's finally going to register me in school.*

I held onto that hope tightly.

But behind her new softness, a plan had already been made — one I knew nothing about.

Two days before it happened, Dominic came to visit for New Year's.
He and Amanda spoke at length behind closed doors. I didn't think much of it.

On Sunday morning, Amanda didn't go to church — only her children did.
She told me to stay back and help her with something in the house.

I didn't suspect anything.

At around 9:30 a.m., I heard a knock on the gate. Then Dominic's voice floated up the stairs:

"The okada man dey wait for me downstairs." This simply means the motorcycle rider is waiting for me downstairs.

Amanda called me from her room.

"Rose!"

"Yes ma." I answered.

"Go and bring your bag. You'll go with Dominic. He will explain everything to you. Your mother sent for you — there's a festival in the village," she said quickly, almost in a hurry.

"Okay ma."

I went to my corner and packed my small Ghana Must Go bag.
I only packed about half of my belongings.

Because I truly believed I was coming back. This was temporary, I thought. A visit.

I didn't get to see the children.

They were still at church.

Amanda didn't call them to say goodbye.

She didn't hug me.

Didn't bless me.

Didn't even walk me to the door.

It was like I had never mattered.

We rode the motorcycle down to Onitsha main car park in silence.

The wind was loud in my ears, but inside, my thoughts were louder.

That's when Dominic told me:

"You're going back to the village."

Just like that.

He wasn't even going with me.

He had way-billed me like a parcel.

I stood at the park and watched as he moved from one driver to another, negotiating transportation fare, explaining to drivers where I will alight.

He paid my fare and handed me off like luggage.

"Once you drop her at the village car park, she knows her way to her mother's place," he told the driver.

And that was it.

Tears filled my eyes.

Not out of fear.

Not even fully out of sadness.

I cried because, for the first time in years, I was going to see my mother. My siblings. My home.

I had been discarded… but I was also going home

Sent Away Without a Word.

By the evening of the same day, I stood in front of my mother's house. My "Ghana-must-go" bag slung over my shoulder.

She opened the door, surprised—really surprised. Her eyes scanned me from head to toe, and confusion filled her face.

"What happened, my daughter? Why have you come back home this time of the year? Will you not go to school again? What will you be doing in this village now? This is January. What about school?" she asked, her voice quick and trembling.

"I don't know," I answered quietly. "They said you wanted me home... for the village festivals."

Tears welled in my eyes. I started crying.

"I didn't send for you," she said, confused. Her voice cracked. Is everything okay?, Did you do anything wrong to your madam?, Why didn't my brother and his wife tell me before sending you back?. They have done wrong".

She held me close. I could feel her trying hard to understand what was happening, but she couldn't stop her own tears. Her voice turned softer:

"It's alright. If others sent you away, I will never send you away. Welcome back home Adam- my daughter. You have suffered enough." She held me and said, "Stop crying. Everything will be alright one day". She always said that when there was nothing else to say.

This was how my second job as a housemaid ended. No goodbyes. No closure—just another chapter closing heavy on my heart. But deep inside, a small spark of hope still lingered, whispering that my story was far from over— better days awaited.

Chapter 9

A Place That Felt Like Home

Mama Joyce's House

My mother didn't have much, but she had her little farm. She grew okra, cassava, corn, and akidi—enough to feed us, but never enough to sell. It was survival farming. That was how we lived.

The day after I returned, I sat beside her, quiet and unsure. "I want to go back to school," I finally said.

She looked at me and nodded slowly, as if she had been thinking the same thing.

"Tomorrow, I'll speak to some of our kinsmen," she said. "Maybe someone will hire me to work on their farm. If I can get paid, you'll go back to school. I promise."

I believed her. My mother had always been known for working hard in other people's farms just to earn a little extra cash. She was respected for that. And she kept her word when she could.

A few days later, she sat beside me again.

"I'll be leaving in a few days," she said. "It's a seven-day job. When I return, you will start school."

I nodded. I held on to that promise like it was a piece of bread.

Then she asked a question I didn't expect.

"Will you stay here with your stepfather, or would you prefer to stay with my elder sister in the next village?". My mother remarried after she and my father separated.

I chose her sister. I didn't know my stepfather well, and I wasn't comfortable around him. Something in me stayed distant from him, even though he had never hurt me. I just didn't feel safe.

Mama Joyce, as we all called her, lived in another village with her husband and six children. I had known them since I was small. I had played with my cousins, eaten in their home, slept under their roof.

Thinking back now, I wonder why I made that choice. Maybe it felt familiar. Maybe it felt less lonely. Maybe I just didn't want to stay with a man I didn't trust. Maybe what happened with Amanda's son played a role.

Preparing to Leave Again.

The night before she left, my mother sat with me and my younger sibling—her last-born, the only child still living with her. All my other siblings had been sent to live with other families as housemaids, just like I had been.

"I've borrowed money to buy foodstuffs that will last you until I return," she said gently. "In the morning, I will take both of you to Mama Joyce's house."

Then she turned to me with a mixture of love and pleading in her eyes.

"Look after your sibling. If my sister or her children annoy you, please endure it. Be patient. Help with house chores. Be obedient."

I nodded. I knew what she meant. I understood more than a child should ever have to.

My Mama's Promise.

Early the next morning, she took us to Mama Joyce's house. She took us by the hand and walked us to Mama Joyce's house. I remember the heaviness in her steps—not just from the bags, but from the weight of leaving her children behind. When we arrived, she gave each of us a long, quiet hug. No tears, no drama. Just a soft, lingering look, like she was memorising our faces.

Then she turned and walked away.

I watched her go, heart aching, holding back tears. I was too young to say it then, but I understood: she was sacrificing everything she had… just so I could have a chance.

She said goodbye, and told me again, "Just seven days."

But seven days turned into more.

And once again, I was in a stranger's home. Once again, I was waiting.

I must tell you this, Mama Joyce and her family were kind.

For the first time in a long time, I felt like part of a household—not a maid, not a burden. We all ate together at the same time. No one set their plates above mine. There were no separate corners for me. I sat with them, like a person.

Every morning at 5:30 a.m., Mama Joyce would gently wake me.

"Nwaogalanyi (as they fondly call me), let's go to the stream."

We would walk together, sometimes in silence, sometimes in conversation. I carried water on my head with a bucket or a gallon and she carried hers, both of us sweating under the rising sun.

She appreciated my help. I remember her saying once, smiling:

"Since you came, I no longer do the dishes. And my water drums have never stayed this full."

That small praise meant more to me than any reward Amanda had ever given. I felt useful. I felt seen.

Chapter 10

Whispers of the Stream

Stream Life

I fetched a lot of water during my time in Mama Joyce's home.

My mother's village had four different streams scattered across the nearby communities. Each stream had its own purpose, its own rhythm, and its own story. There was Ogbu, Tabasi, Ogolujo, Ahala—known for its sweet water—and others like Ube and Omabala.

There was one called Ogbu. The taste of the water is different from other streams. The path to the stream was straight and not lonely, unlike the winding, narrow bush roads that led to others. The water from Ogbu wasn't very sweet, so we didn't drink it. It was used mainly for cooking, washing clothes, and bathing.

The water from Ogbu wasn't sweet, so we didn't drink it. It was used mostly for cooking, washing clothes, and bathing.

One thing I'll never forget about Ogbu is a story my mother and her older sister, Mama Joyce, told me after I asked about the fishes and the strange man-made gods I'd seen along the road.

I remember asking why the fishes I saw swimming so freely weren't being caught and cooked like the ones from other streams.

My mother explained that those fishes belonged to Ogbu. Ogbu is an *Alusi*—a spiritual deity, seen by the villagers as a *chi*, or god. Although more than seventy percent of the villagers weren't religious in the conventional sense, they believed deeply in the man-made god. They revered and obeyed it with unwavering respect.

Sacrifices and rituals were offered to Ogbu during times of need—when someone was ill, when crops failed, when there was injustice or conflict in the village, or even when someone went missing.

Hearing this as a child filled me with awe, shock, and a quiet fear. The idea that the fishes were sacred—untouchable—made me terrified of accidentally harming one. It felt like more than just a stream; Ogbu was alive, watching.

The water we fetched early in the morning was Ahala and Tabasi, however, was different—cool, fresh, and sweet. That was the drinking water. We made sure to get it before the sun grew too high.

Sometimes I followed Mama Joyce to the farms to gather firewood. Other times, I stayed back to help in the kitchen. She never treated me like a slave. She gave me responsibilities, but not punishment. She gave me chores, but not cruelty.

Her kindness, simple as it was, stayed with me. It taught me that work didn't have to mean suffering. That family could be firm but fair. That not everyone who took a child into their home meant to break them.

But even as I settled into this small peace, I knew it couldn't last forever. My mother had promised to return after seven days.

And I was still waiting. It's already a month by this time.

The Man by the Stream.

One afternoon, I was coming out of the Ogbu stream, balancing water on my head, when I saw a man walking toward me.

We greeted politely. Then he asked, "Whose daughter are you?"

I ignored the question, but I told him my name.

"You're not from this village," he said. "Ihite-Ogwari is small. We know when someone new is among us. Who are your parents? Why aren't you in school?"

I looked at him quietly, then kept walking.

But he followed me. All the way to Mama Joyce's compound.

I was nervous. I had planned to return to the stream for more water, but I abandoned the idea. My heart was pounding. I didn't know why he followed me, or what he wanted. But I had a strange feeling I would see him again.

That evening, after dinner, I told Mama Joyce everything that had happened.

She looked confused.

"What name did he say?" she asked.

"Clem," I replied.

She frowned.

"That's not an Igbo name. We don't know any 'Clem' here."

In the village, people were known by their native names—Igbo names. English names didn't help much, especially with strangers.

Clem Returns.

Two days later, I went out again to fetch water. And there he was—Clem—standing by the road that led to the Ogbu stream.

"Don't be afraid," he said gently. "I live in this village too. I just want to know who your parents are."

"I'm a daughter to Mama Joyce," I said firmly. "And I'm from this village."

He looked at me and shook his head.

"You're not telling the truth, and you know it. Mama Joyce has only one daughter. She's grown and married. The rest are all boys."

He was right. I stayed silent.

"So who are you, really?" he asked again.

I paused, then replied, "Mama Joyce is my big aunty. I'm staying with her for now."

"I knew it," he said. "Besides, you don't act like someone from this village."

Then he told me his story.

"I live in Lagos. I only came home for the Christmas and New Year holidays. I'll be going back in three days. There's a woman in Lagos—Madam Gold. She's looking for a young girl to help in her house and care for her children. You'll be a housemaid. But she's Igbo too. If you're interested, you can come with me."

I looked at him, cautious.

"Will she send me to school?"

"Yes. She's willing to train you if you're serious about your education."

"Please speak to Mama Joyce first," I said.

"I will come this evening," he promised.

We parted ways at the bend in the road. He went his way, and I returned home, thinking.

Chapter 11

A New Beginning…or So I Thought

A New Opportunity

That evening, after we finished eating, I told Mama Joyce everything Clem had said. I told her he planned to come that night to speak with her and her husband.

She listened, then nodded. She knew my mother wasn't home. She was responsible for me now.

Around 9 p.m., Clem arrived. He spoke with Mama Joyce and her husband about the possibility of taking me to Lagos to work for Madam Gold. They listened carefully.

Later, Mama Joyce sat me down and repeated what had been discussed. Then she asked me directly:

"Do you really want to go to Lagos?"

"Yes," I said.

Because the truth was, I saw no other way forward except school. And if this was the road that could lead me back into a classroom, I was ready to take it. Even if it meant starting over again. Even if it meant becoming someone's maid again.

In that moment, I remembered my mother—why she left, what she carried on her shoulders, and the sacrifices she made.

"She will understand," I said to myself.

And so, I prepared for another journey.

A Journey of Hope and Uncertainty.

As soon as Mama Joyce gave her consent for me to travel with Clem, I packed my belongings that night to avoid any delays in the morning.

I used a medium-sized, chequered plastic bag—what people call a "Ghana-Must-Go." It was noisy and rough, but it held everything I owned. I remember Mama Joyce asking why I packed so many clothes.

"Don't worry about all that," she said. "Madam Gold will buy you new clothes."

But I didn't believe her. I had learned by now that promises were often not kept. So I packed what little I had.

What bothered me more was leaving without my mother's approval. I hadn't seen her or spoken to her. I was worried she'd be angry. But deep down, I trusted that since Mama Joyce supported it, my mother would understand. Before we left, I begged Mama Joyce and Clem to explain everything to her when she returned.

Leaving the Village.

The next morning, Mama Joyce walked with me to the bus garage to meet Clem.

Even though I had eaten breakfast, she gave me ₦20 to buy food on the way.

As she handed me over, she looked at Clem and said quietly:

"Remember all that we discussed."

We boarded a long-distance bus heading toward the city. I didn't know where we were going, or how far it was. As a child, I simply followed Clem and trusted him to lead the way. The journey was confusing—we took three buses and several motorcycles (Okadas). I didn't know the names of the towns we passed through.

The journey to Lagos didn't happen all at once. It lasted nearly four days.

A Strange Stop.

Along the way, Clem and I stopped at a house belonging to one of his friends. We stayed there for two nights. I counted the days by the number of times we slept there.

The man's wife-to-be was kind and spoke to me in general Igbo, though the man and Clem spoke in my mother's dialect. The woman was welcoming and homely. They lived in a single room, but she cooked for us and made me feel safe.

She even encouraged me to rest in the afternoons, telling me gently:

"Go and lie down, my dear. Rest while I rest."

But despite the warmth, I couldn't relax.

I kept asking Clem, "Is this Lagos?"

"No," he would reply. "Don't worry. We'll leave for Lagos tomorrow. I'm sorting something out."

His answers didn't satisfy me. I was young, but not foolish. I began to suspect something wasn't right. I didn't know Clem very well before traveling with him, and I had no way of contacting anyone. Still, Mama Joyce had trusted him. She had told me:

"Clem is a good man. His parents are respected. He has a good reputation."

One night, I overheard Clem talking to his friend about money. I believed he had run out of money, which may have been why we stayed there longer than expected. To this day, I'm still not certain why we stopped there at all.

Arriving in Lagos.

On Day 3, we finally left and reached Lagos early Sunday morning, in February 2007.

We took an Okada from the last bus stop to Clem's place. He lived in a single room inside someone else's flat.

When we arrived, Clem left me alone in the room to go and buy bread. He returned after a long while.

"Shops are all closed," he explained. "It's Sunday. I couldn't find fresh bread. We'll have to manage this until tomorrow."

He made tea for both of us using a kettle—I didn't know how to use it, so he did it himself. He served me Agege bread with butter and a hot cup of tea.

Clem was respectful and considerate during my stay with him. For the first two nights, I slept in his room. But I soon began to worry.

He would leave me alone at home while he went to work. Each day, I asked him:

"When will you take me to Madam Gold?"

"I've been calling her," he'd reply. "She hasn't answered yet. Once she does, I'll take you there."

I grew uneasy. I didn't want to stay long in a stranger's house.

Finally, one evening, he came home with news:

"I've spoken to Madam Gold. She said she'll be home on Thursday. That's when I'll take you."

I felt a wave of hope.

"She'll still put me in school, right?" I asked.

"Yes. That's part of the agreement," he confirmed. "She has money. You'll be very happy there."

Holding Onto Hope.

I was excited. I had a dream—to become a graduate. No one in my family had finished secondary school, let alone reached university. I wanted to change that.

I promised myself that I would do well in school. I imagined showing off my report card to Madam Gold—and later, to my mother.

"She'll be proud," I told myself.

I also knew that the second term of school had just started. If I began now, I wouldn't be too far behind. I could still catch up.

So I waited for Thursday, full of hope.

Chapter 12

Behind Her Smile

The House of Many Faces

The day came for me to meet her. Clem, as usual, gave me instructions: I would be caring for Joel, her newborn baby, and doing household chores. He described the home like a small boarding house—full of family, friends, a maid called Nkechi, and cousins who came and went.

I was nervous but hopeful. Clem assured me he'd check in once in a while. That gave me a little courage.

Meeting Madam Gold.
We arrived around 11:30 a.m. Nkechi welcomed us in, then went to call Madam Gold. The house smelled of polish and perfume. Her living room had framed photographs, plush cushions, and a quiet that didn't match the number of people Clem had described.

She greeted us warmly and served cold Coke and Fanta with biscuits. I watched her—elegant, smiling, composed. Her kindness surprised me. I stood up and greeted her: "Good morning, Ma."

"Good morning. Please sit down."

While she and Clem spoke, I admired the photos on the wall—her husband (she said he was in London), baby pictures, and stylish portraits of herself. But I was also listening, trying to catch if school was part of the plan.

She finally turned to me:

"You will be responsible for Joel. He's your job now. If anything happens to him, I'll hold you responsible."

I nodded. That was the official beginning of my third housemaid job.

The First Test.
As they talked, Joel started crying. Nkechi tried to soothe him, but nothing worked. Madam Gold grew visibly upset. I offered to carry him. Nkechi hesitated, then asked,

"Aunty, should I let her carry the baby?"

"Yes," Madam Gold replied.

The moment I held him, Joel stopped crying and fell asleep. That was my quiet victory—my unspoken introduction.

After Clem left, Madam Gold laid down the rules. I would care for Joel, clean the house, wash clothes, cook, mop, sweep, clean windows, and wash her car. Nkechi and her cousin would handle Larry and assist in the house too.

Madam Gold ran a Mary Kay business. Her sister in America sent boxes of products, and every morning she packed them and left the house, returning late—sometimes past 7 p.m.

One day, I overheard one of her cousins crying to Nkechi:

"She doesn't help me. Even as her sister, I've been living with her for years without support. No salary. Nothing." She wept. Nkechi comforted her and shared her own pain. "I've been here before Larry was born. She promised me school. Years have passed. I've seen nothing. I don't think it'll ever happen."

That shook me.

The House When She's Gone.
Something else became clear. When Madam Gold left for the day, the house changed. People laughed, played music, and sat comfortably. Nkechi would stretch out on the couch, and the tension in the house dissolved.

There were jollof rice "emergency" cookouts, whispers, and temporary joy.

But the moment we heard her car at the gate, everything changed. Silence returned. Everyone snapped back to their roles. Fear took its place in the living room.

In our street, people called her a troublemaker. She brags about this, too. Inside her house, she was the storm everyone was afraid to name.

Dreams on Hold.
The first week in Madam Gold's house passed in a blur. I woke early, before the sun, and slept late, often after everyone else had gone to bed. Every day, I was busy — feeding Joel, changing him, washing baby clothes, mopping floors, scrubbing bathrooms, cooking, and running errands. There was no space left for my own thoughts.

But still, I held on to one thing: school.

She had promised. Clem had promised. And I believed them.

"I'll look for a school nearby," Madam Gold had said. *"Just settle in first."*

So I waited.

A Long Wait.

Days became weeks. Each time I asked about school, she brushed it off.

"Not now. I've been too busy. Don't worry, I haven't forgotten."

But it felt like she had.

Nkechi told me, "She said the same thing to me years ago. I'm still waiting."

I didn't want to believe that would be my story too. I worked even harder, thinking maybe if she saw my commitment, she would keep her promise.

She didn't.

Joel became my entire world. I carried him on my back as I cleaned. When he cried, I sang softly to him. I watched him smile, grow, and take his first steps. He knew me more than he knew his mother.

One evening, Madam Gold returned from her Mary Kay rounds and found a stain on Joel's shirt.

"What is this?" she snapped.

"It must've been when I fed him Cerelac. He spilled a little."

She slapped me.

It wasn't just the slap — it was the disappointment. That this woman who smiled at me on my first day, who gave me biscuits and Fanta, could raise her hand at me like I was nothing.

No apology. No explanation. Just instructions:

"Next time, make sure he's clean before I return."

I nodded, eyes full but lips sealed.

In that house, there were many of us — working, surviving, holding in pain. Nkechi had her own battle. Her cousin, a quiet young adult, often stared blankly into space. I didn't know her full story, but I saw the same tiredness in her eyes that I began to feel in mine.

There were children like me in other flats too — housemaids — walking barefoot to the communal tap, carrying babies, sweeping courtyards. I began to understand something quietly: this was not just my life. This was normal.

But just because it was common didn't mean it was right.

Where Is Clem?.
Weeks passed, and Clem never returned. I had so many questions. Did he forget me? Was he afraid to face what he had left me in?

I asked Madam Gold one day,

"Have you heard from Clem?"

"Mind your business. Focus on your work," she said.

That was the last time I mentioned his name.

At night, when the house was finally quiet and the children were asleep, I would stare at the ceiling and whisper:

"One day, I will go to school. One day, this will end."

But a small voice in my head had started to ask,

What if it doesn't?

I didn't let that voice win. Not yet.

Chapter 13

The House of Broken Promises

Caged Dreams: A Child's Fight for Education

I arrived at Madam Gold's house on February 12th, 2007, an almost nine to ten-year-old girl with dreams of school and a future. The agreement was simple: I would perform daily chores and responsibilities, and in return, she would pay for my secondary school education. I never received a salary, and I never knew if Clem, the man who arranged this for me, was paid.

Lagos was vast and intimidating, its streets unfamiliar and noisy. The house where I lived was full of strangers, yet I had to navigate its rules, fears, and dangers as if I belonged. Months passed without a word about school. I didn't know whether to ask or wait. I remembered Nkechi's story—how she had been kept from school—but I refused to let it discourage me. Education was everything. I promised myself: it would be education or nothing.

One morning, Madam Gold seemed unusually cheerful. She laughed freely on the phone and treated everyone around her kindly. I saw a small window of hope. "Aunty, when will I start school?" I asked. "You said you would call the schools so I could register."

Her response was like a stone dropping in my chest: "I couldn't register you. Let's wait until next term because you've already missed the start of this one." I nodded silently, returning to my chores, but inside, a storm of frustration and fear raged. I knew she could make it happen if she wanted. Our neighbour's daughter, the same age as me, had no trouble enrolling.

Later, while washing clothes, our neighbour asked why I wasn't in school. I explained my situation, and she encouraged me: "You could still catch up." I thought of Clem, but I didn't have his contact details or know his address. I swallowed my disappointment and continued working, quietly clinging to the hope of schooling.

By August 2007, Madam Gold announced that the new school term would start in a month and her son would advance to a new class. I approached her the next day. "Aunty, I wanted to know if you were able to register me in school as the new term begins in a month."

Her response was swift and terrifying. She slapped me across the face and shouted, "The next time you ask me questions about school, you will see how I deal with you! Get out of my sight!" I ran to the second room, shaking and crying.

Nkechi, a woman almost seventeen years my senior who had endured Madam Gold's cruelty before me, hugged me and whispered, "Be strong. Stop crying. If Aunty hears you, she will beat you even more. You have to be strong."

I realised I was not alone in my suffering, but fear consumed me.

Madam Gold discovered I had spoken to Clem about her actions when he called the house phone. Furious, she threw my bag outside and forced me into the cold Lagos night. I had no one. No family, no friends. The streets were huge and unwelcoming.

Neighbours tried to help, but Madam Gold's anger was terrifying. I spent the night outside, shivering, with baby Joel crying inside. His cries pierced the night, and I could hear Madam Gold shouting at Nkechi for failing to soothe him.

The next morning, Jade, a cousin, arrived and asked me to run an errand. I refused, afraid of Madam Gold's wrath. Jade pleaded, but it was clear Madam Gold's anger would not be appeased.

Nkechi brought me lunch later, urging me to plead for forgiveness. I knelt, apologised repeatedly, and begged to return inside. Reluctantly, she allowed it—but my punishment continued. I slept outside again that night, the baby crying intermittently, each wail a reminder of my vulnerability.

The next morning, Madam Gold pulled me inside by my ear, commanding me to bathe, change, and carry Joel. Even then, she monitored me, slapping me if I hesitated. Yet, in caring for the baby, I found a strange bond. I soothed him like no one else could.

Time passed. By the next visit from Clem, Madam Gold had softened slightly. She admitted she had taken out her frustrations on me and offered a small apology. She promised a trip to London for her family and said I would start school when we returned. Naïve, I believed her.

I was only ten. My mind raced: *Where is London? How long will we be there? Will I finally go to school?* Fear and uncertainty weighed heavily, but I dared not ask.

When Clem visited, I confided in him about the abuse and months lost to fear and neglect. He was shocked and worried. "What if an animal had attacked you? What if you were killed?" he asked. But I could not tell him about London. Madam Gold had warned me to remain silent.

After Clem left, Madam Gold confronted me, demanding to know what I had said. I lied as instructed. Her anger was immediate, and I feared punishment.

That night, as I lay on the thin mat, my mind wandered. I was a ten-year-old girl trapped between fear and hope, longing for education, longing for safety, longing for a life that seemed just out of reach.

A Home of Conflict.

From the moment Nkechi and I noticed tension with Madam Gold, life became unpredictable. One day, she summoned me to her room and said sharply:

"Nkechi will no longer take care of Larry. From tomorrow, you will manage everything concerning my children. Nkechi will continue with her other chores."

I replied, "Okay, Aunty," and left. The next day, I took over both children's care, but Nkechi's sadness was palpable. She was tearful, withdrawn, and no longer herself. When her relative intervened, pleading with Madam Gold to honour promises about schooling and fair treatment, Madam Gold refused to compromise. That evening, she forced Nkechi out of the house, tossing her belongings in a small bag. Nkechi left, defeated and heartbroken.

With Nkechi gone, the full burden fell on me. Life became grueling:

Nights:
I would wake repeatedly to feed, bathe, and soothe Joel,

whose colic often left him inconsolable. I slept on the bare concrete floor, wrapped in a single piece of African fabric. Cramped, aching, and cold—sometimes I woke up with rat bites on my toes. Sleep deprivation led to headaches, dizziness, and constant fatigue.

Mornings:
At 5:30 AM, I would fetch water from the borehole, sweep the house, wash dishes, cook meals, iron school uniforms, prepare lunchboxes, bathe the children, and take Larry to school. Carrying Joel on my back while managing chores left little time to rest or eat. My morning meals often didn't come until 2 p.m. Hunger became part of the routine.

Emotional Toll:

Watching children my age in school deepened my sadness. Yet, I clung to one goal: education. Despite exhaustion and mistreatment, I refused to accept the life planned for most girls in my village—early marriage, labour, and little or no schooling.

Madam Gold's punishments were harsh and unpredictable.

One evening, she sent me to buy pepper soup from the nearby shop. It was rush hour, and the woman selling the soup told me to wait—she knew Madam Gold preferred it freshly made, and a new pot was still cooking.

By the time I returned, Madam Gold was already waiting. The look on her face told me I was in trouble. I could hear baby Joel crying inside the house.

I tried to explain, but she didn't care. She grabbed me and reached for her big rainbow-coloured umbrella—then beat me with it until it shattered.

She continued with slapping, pinching and punching. Joel's cries grew louder, but she ignored them as she struck me again and again. When it was finally over, I was left with bruises and swelling on my eyes, lips, and belly. I could barely walk. I was ordered to sweep the pieces off the floor.

I still have the mark on my palm to this day.

Witnesses, like Ms Uloma, tried to intervene, but Madam Gold threatened her. Yet, I endured, believing that education was worth any hardship.

Chapter 14

Crossing Borders, Carrying Burdens

Preparation for the UK

Madam Gold decided I would accompany her and the children to London without asking my consent. My parents were not informed either. Clem was not aware either. If they knew, I would have been informed. I was coerced into lying about my identity: she would be my stepmother, my mother was "dead," and the children were my stepbrothers.

I was prepared meticulously:

- Haircuts for myself and Larry.
- Photographs and thumbprints for passports.
- Special travel clothing.

Despite the careful planning, I was terrified and confused. I did not understand where I was going or why my voice was ignored.

The Journey.

We left Nigeria on the night of 31st December 2007. This was ten months of living with Madam Gold. Multiple flights, long layovers, cold weather, and hunger marked the journey. I was constantly monitored, punished for resting, and had to care for the children throughout. By the time we landed in London on 2nd January 2008, I was exhausted, shivering, and barely able to walk.

Arrival in London.

Instead of a home, we went to the house of Ms Tega, a friend of Madam Gold. She was welcoming but knew I was not Madam Gold's daughter. While Madam Gold worked at a Launderette three times a week, I continued caring for Larry and Joel, adapting to the cold weather and new environment. Despite the brief comfort, I remained under strict supervision, and my autonomy was limited.

The abuse continued the moment we arrived in the UK. We were staying at Ms Tega's house when Madam Gold's cruelty returned with full force. We lived there for about a month, but tension built between Madam Gold and Ms Tega, her former friend. One incident between Madam Gold and me ignited that tension.

One day, without warning, Madam Gold struck me with her high-heeled shoe. I have forgotten what I had done wrong. Pain exploded across my body as she beat me mercilessly. My head and face swelled, and scratches from her fingernails bled down my neck. I was left with open wounds and shock coursing through me.

Then she dragged me outside and locked the door behind me. I stood in the freezing January air with only stockings on my feet, no jacket, shivering violently. I knocked again and again, desperate for mercy. Hours passed. My teeth chattered. My fingers felt numb. Panic clawed at my chest. I didn't know what to do.

Finally, I ran to Ms Tega's shop. She looked at me and froze. Her face hardened in anger and disbelief.

"Madam Gold did this to you?"

I could not answer. Fear paralysed my voice. Ms Tega's eyes blazed as she exclaimed:

"Will she treat her own children like this? This is someone else's child!"

She grabbed her mobile phone and called Madam Gold.

"Do you want to kill this girl? How can you beat her like this? This will not happen in my house again. If you ever treat her like this next time, I will call the police on you."

After the call, she turned to me:

"Go home. I don't think she will touch you again."

I obeyed, walking back to the house with fear coiling in my stomach. Weeks passed. I noticed Madam Gold stayed home more often. She no longer went to the Launderette. She moved silently, packing things and disappearing upstairs to make and receive phone calls. I didn't realise then that she was preparing for our next move.

On the evening of 30th January 2008, she brought our luggage downstairs. That night, we left Ms Tega's house in a large black car. I didn't see Ms Tega again to say "thank you" or "goodbye." My heart pounded, filled with fear and uncertainty. Where were we going? What awaited us next?

The car stopped, and I stepped out into the cold, uncertain of what awaited us. We were thirty minutes from Ms Tega's house, now heading to Mama Ada's home in Haggerston, just opposite the 'Snake Park' in Hackney. I had no idea why we were moving again.

When we arrived, Madam Gold introduced me as her daughter. Mama Ada greeted us warmly in Igbo, my mother tongue:

"Madam Gold, I did not know you have a daughter of this age," she said. "I knew of your two little sons, but not a girl as old as Rose."

Madam Gold explained quickly:

"She is my step-daughter. She is my husband's daughter. Her mother is dead, so I decided to bring her with me to London."

I froze, confused and scared. Daughter or step-daughter? I didn't know. Each word felt like a trap. When Mama Ada noticed the scratches on my face and neck, my throat went dry. I could not speak. Madam Gold's threats were always close.

Mama Ada's daughters were kind, offering smiles and gentle words. That first night, I slept on the wooden floor in the living room, wrapped in bed covers, while the children and their mother shared the sofas. Later, we moved upstairs to a room with a bunk bed, belonging to one of Mama Ada's daughters who was travelling to Nigeria for two weeks. I took the top bunk—Madam Gold insisted her sons must not catch a cold.

One quiet day, when Mama Ada stayed home, she asked me to help tidy the house. Then she handed me some clothes to try on. As I changed, she gently held my hand and asked me to sit down. Looking at me closely, she asked:

"Where did all these marks come from? Did Madam Gold do this to you?"

Fear froze me. I could barely speak.

"Rose, talk to me. This is too much."

"I cannot tell you," I whispered.

"Why?"

"Because she will know if I tell someone," I said.

Finally, I confided in her, telling everything. Mama Ada confronted Madam Gold, who denied it and claimed I was exaggerating. Mama Ada calmly explained:

"I had no choice but to speak to her. This is not Nigeria. She cannot abuse you here. It is unacceptable in my house or in the UK."

Weeks passed. Madam Gold started working again, though I didn't know the exact job. I noticed she always carried a white and red kitchen apron in her bag. One day, Mama Ada advised her to register Larry in the nursery school behind her house. That week, Larry began attending nursery for the first time—a small victory amid the uncertainty.

I had been at Mama Ada's house for about a month when the process of getting me into school began. Mama Ada had pressured Madam Gold, insisting that a child of school age could not remain out of school in the UK. She explained firmly:

"It is against the law for a child of school age not to be in school."

Madam Gold was furious. She shouted, cursed, and verbally abused me. Each word left my chest heavy with fear, but Mama Ada remained unshaken:

"Any child staying in my house will go to school."

Mama Ada began making arrangements for my enrollment. I sat nervously in the living room as she called several secondary schools near her home to check for available spaces. One school had none, but Clapton Girls Technology College, where a friend of hers worked, had a spot in Year 8. I was accepted, and an interview was scheduled for me, accompanied by a person with parental responsibility.

The same day, I overheard Mama Ada explaining the interview details to Madam Gold. As always, Madam Gold found a way to complicate things:

"I cannot make the interview," she said, probably because she was working.

I realized then that she often gave me payslips in another woman's name to deliver elsewhere—her ways to stay hidden and control the story.

On the day of the interview, Madam Gold woke me abruptly and reminded me of what I must say:

"Remember to tell them I'm your step-mother, and that your mother is dead."

I nodded silently, my stomach twisting with unease. I knew my mother was alive, but Madam Gold had never met her. I was trapped in her fabricated story.

Mama Ada accompanied me to the school. Every step felt heavy, my mind racing with fear. Would Madam Gold make things difficult? Would the school believe me? Thankfully, the interview went smoothly, and I was told I would start school the following week, on 10th March 2008. By this time, it had been one year and two weeks since I began living with Madam Gold.
Indeed, the journey ahead had already been foretold by the prophetess.
Who would have believed I would have to endure so much hardship and suffering before I could even start school?. I thought it would be straightforward. I thank God for perseverance.

Two days before the school start date, Madam Gold took me to a nearby charity shop. She bought me second-hand black trouser and a worn pair of shoes, while Mama Ada had already bought my school polo. Standing in the shop, I felt a mixture of excitement and dread. For the first time, I would walk into a school as a student, but the shadow of Madam Gold's control lingered.

On my first day, the school asked for my passport and proof of address. I did not have these, and my heart pounded as they called Madam Gold to bring them. I was left in the waiting room, unable to enter the classroom. Every passing second felt like an eternity. I watched every passerby, imagining the worst.

When Madam Gold finally arrived, I held my breath. She handed over my Nigerian passport, and the staff quickly made a photocopy. Through the reception window, I saw the details for the first time. Growing up in a poor family in Nigeria, birthdays were hardly celebrated. My mother never told me, and I had never asked. Seeing it in print felt unreal.

For the first time in months, a small spark of hope stirred inside me. I was going to school. I remembered my favourite quote, "He that started a good work in my life will complete it". I held my breath for seconds with my eyes closed and exhaled. I could finally start learning, and maybe, just maybe, a different life was beginning.

The brief moment I believed freedom was mine.

I was finally happy to have started going to school. After years of chaos and being treated like a house girl, this felt like a very big victory. I was extremely excited.

Madam Gold was never really happy about me attending school. I started in Year 8. We were still living in Hackney, at Mama Ada's house, for about a month and a half.

When Mama Ada could no longer support us because her daughter was returning from Nigeria, we had to leave. While we were there, I looked after Larry and Joel. Madam Gold still treated me as the house girl, but Mama Ada and her children noticed and often said it was wrong to treat a child that way.

We then moved to Ancis House, a council flat beside Britannia Leisure Centre in Islington. It had four rooms, each rented to someone else. Madam Gold and Larry shared a bed while Joel and I slept on the floor. We shared the kitchen and bathroom with the other tenants.

Ancis House was about a ten-minute walk from Mama Ada's home. I would get a bus to school in the mornings. Madam Gold worked nights and during the day, always carrying her uniform in a bag. Larry had just started school, around four or five years old.

My mornings began at 5:30 a.m. I bathed the children, dressed them, fed them breakfast, and then dropped Larry at school and took Joel to a childminder near Kingsmead Primary School before I could leave for my own classes. Most mornings, I had no time to eat before heading to school.

Larry attended Queensbridge Primary School, starting two weeks before me. From the very beginning, I was responsible for dropping him off and picking him up. The first day, I went with Mama Ada's daughter.
Because I was at school full days and Larry only attended half days, Madam Gold arranged for another Nigerian woman, Flora, to look after him in the afternoons. This began in March 2008 while we were still at Mama Ada's house.

After we moved to Ancis House, Flora helped even more. She offered to take Larry in the mornings so I could drop Joel off first without being late. I would carry Joel on my back with a wrapper, walk 20–30 minutes to Flora's house, then continue to the childminder before catching the bus to school.
Before Flora helped, I was always late for school. I wrote false reasons for being late, fearing Madam Gold's reaction if anyone knew I was taking care of the children.

Most of the time when I wasn't at school, I looked after Joel while Madam Gold went out with Larry. Even on rare trips with her or at church, my role as house girl was obvious. Flora noticed my stress and sometimes helped, giving me small breaks and support.

One day, Flora told Madam Gold that carrying Joel on my back every day was too much and could damage my back. Madam Gold reluctantly agreed to get a pushchair for him.

Even in these small moments of relief, I realised that happiness was fleeting. Every day was a balancing act of survival, responsibility, and hope. Attending school gave me a sense of freedom, but the reality of life with Madam Gold always hovered close behind.

Chapter 15

The First Glimpse of Hope

First Police Incident

When fear met the law—but protection was fleeting.

Sometime between late May and early June 2008, everything changed—the police got involved for the first time.

It was a Sunday morning, around 5:30 a.m. Larry had woken up early and decided to start eating ice cream he'd taken from the freezer. I told him it was too early and I asked him to stop. I attempted taking it away severally but every time I tried, he insisted he could do whatever he wanted.

Then he turned up the volume on the television, waking Joel, who joined him in eating ice cream. Larry went back to the fridge for water—and a cold bottle of Coke.

I tried to stop them, but they didn't listen. Madam Gold was sleeping and hates being disturbed. Suddenly, both began vomiting and complained of stomach pains. I panicked and woke Madam Gold. She checked them and discovered they were very hot—they must have had a fever. She instructed me to get a bowl of cold water and a towel, and she cooled them down. Eventually, they calmed and fell asleep.

Violence Strikes.

Even when the boys were safe, my own safety was not guaranteed. Madam Gold turned her fury on me, pushing, kicking, and punching. She slammed my head against the wall socket twice, breaking it into two. Her long nails tore my ear, drawing blood. She yelled that I had wished her children dead and that everything was my fault.

When she left the house for the market, I realised asking for help could be dangerous but necessary. I left Joel at home and ran to Flora's house. I explained everything—Madam Gold's attack, her threats, and my fear—and told Flora I wanted to call the police. Theresa's words echoed in my mind: the police could protect me. Flora asked if I was sure. I said yes. Using her phone, I called and explained that Madam Gold, my stepmother, had attacked me.

When the police arrived, I immediately told them Joel was still home. They took us back to the house to understand the situation. By that time, Madam Gold had returned. After hearing my account, they took Larry, Joel, and me to Homerton Hospital for checks. My ear was bleeding. I was kept for hours for treatment.

For a brief moment, hope appeared. I was placed in foster care for two days and assigned a social worker. I was separated from the boys but felt safer than I had in a long time.
Soon, the police informed me that Madam Gold was very sorry and I could return home. Fear gripped me—I knew she had threatened to punish me for calling them. I told them, but it didn't matter. I was sent back into her care.

Madam Gold made sure I understood the consequences. She shouted that I had caused trouble with the police and that all her details were now known. She reminded me of her threats: I would suffer, she would be protected, and her lawyer friends would ensure her safety. I realised that outside intervention was fragile, and my survival depended on navigating her control.

Flora, having overheard me tell the police I was only Madam Gold's stepdaughter, began helping more. She gave me breakfast before school and prepared food for us after school. She handled shopping for Madam Gold so I wouldn't have to. During weekends and school holidays, she took me, Larry, and Joel into her home, offering rare moments of care and normalcy.

From that day on, I learned that protection could be temporary. The police could intervene, but Madam Gold's control and threats continued. School and the small kindnesses from people like Flora became my only refuge. Every day taught me how to survive, balancing fear, responsibility, and the hope of one day finding true safety.

Flora's Kindness.
The woman who fed me when my own "family" starved me.
After the first police incident, Flora began to see me differently. She realised I wasn't Madam Gold's daughter but her stepchild. She quietly offered small acts of kindness that made a huge difference in my life.

Flora started giving me breakfast before school, ensuring I had at least one proper meal in the morning. She also prepared food for Larry, Joel, and me when we returned from school, so we weren't left hungry after long, exhausting days.

When I had shopping to do, Flora instructed me to give her the list and money. She would do the shopping during the day so that when I returned from school, everything was ready. It was a small relief, but it made my days far less stressful.

A Safe Haven.

On weekends and during school holidays, Flora sometimes took us into her home. Sometimes all three of us stayed with her for two weeks at a time. Other times, it was just me and one of the boys. These stays gave me rare moments of safety and normalcy, away from Madam Gold's constant control and abuse.

A Teacher of Survival

Flora also became a guide, showing me that kindness exists even in the darkest circumstances. She never scolded or punished me; instead, she quietly observed my struggles and offered support when she could. Her actions taught me that survival sometimes depends on finding the people who quietly help you, even when the world seems against you.

The First Glimpse of Hope

For the first time, I began to see that life could be different. Although Madam Gold still dominated every part of my life, Flora's presence gave me hope and a glimpse of the care I had been missing. Her small gestures reminded me that there were people willing to fight for me in ways Madam Gold never would.

Eviction & Hostels.
Losing a home, but never escaping Madam Gold's grip.
On October 31, 2009, the day before Larry's birthday, the landlord arrived at Ancis House with two others to evict us because Madam Gold had refused to pay the rent. A birthday cake for Larry sat untouched, and the clothes she had bought for him hung in the closet.

Conflict in the Street.

Madam Gold immediately clashed with the landlord. A physical altercation broke out in front of our flat. Fear gripped me, but Madam Gold ordered me to call the police and explain what was happening. I did as I was told, trembling as the authorities arrived.

The police asked Madam Gold if she had friends she could stay with. She didn't, so they helped us move our belongings to the Metropolitan Hostel along Kingsland Road. We stayed there for about three days—a brief respite from the chaos of eviction, but hardly a home.

From the hostel, we moved to stay with Madam Gold's friend, Olu, a nurse in Tottenham. We lived there for three to four months until January 2010. It was a one-bedroom flat, and the space was tight.

There was a connection between Olu's family and Larry. Her brother's wife had children living in the UK, while the brother remained in Nigeria. At some point, the police became involved when the brother tried to retrieve his children, though I was not involved in the situation.

Despite the changes in address, my life did not improve. Madam Gold reminded me constantly that if I wanted I could return to Nigeria—but only if she agreed. The one time in 2009 I said I wanted to go, she beat me and yelled that I owed her for bringing me to the UK. I had no way to contact my family in Nigeria and so had no choice but to stay.

Even at Olu's flat, I remained the house girl—cleaning, cooking, and obeying. My life revolved around serving others while I continued attending school whenever I could.

Every day was a balancing act, trying to survive in a world where I had no control over my own life.

At Olu's one-bedroom flat, life was cramped and uncomfortable. If she wasn't working at night, she slept in the bed with Larry and Joel, and I slept on the floor. Despite the change in location, my role as house girl never ended.

The nurse noticed how poorly Madam Gold treated me and offered advice. She suggested that I could change my name back to my grandfather's name, to show that I wasn't related to Madam Gold. I went to school and spoke to the safeguarding teachers, who told me it wasn't possible.

In January 2010, Madam Gold said her lawyer had arranged a new place for us—Spring Lodge Hotel by Seven Sisters Road. We stayed there until June. Life continued as normal. Madam Gold continued working throughout this time, and I continued attending school while also serving as a house girl.

After leaving Spring Lodge Hotel, we moved to Anchodale House in Hackney. It was a two-bedroom flat, but Madam Gold rented the second bedroom to another man. A family friend of Madam Gold also stayed with us, sleeping in the living room. I continued to attend school while managing all household responsibilities.

Chapter 16

The Endless Cycle

The Endless Cycle.

No matter where we moved, no matter the temporary relief, my life remained the same: work, care for Larry and Joel, and obey Madam Gold. School was my only escape, my only hope. Survival was never easy, and every day reminded me that independence and safety were still far away.

Learning, surviving, and finding small wins in a life of fear.

Even after the first police incident, life continued under Madam Gold's control. I returned to school, exhausted and emotionally drained, but determined not to let my education slip away. It became my sanctuary—the one place where I could imagine a life beyond the chaos at home.

I became careful about what I said and did. Madam Gold's constant threats meant I had to hide my fears, lie about lateness, and manage the children's needs without drawing attention. Each day taught me resilience and the subtle art of survival.

There were rare moments of victory: completing a challenging school assignment, receiving praise from a teacher, or having a quiet conversation with Flora. These small successes reminded me that despite the abuse and constant work at home, I still could grow, learn, and hope for a better future.

Even in the darkest days, I began to recognise that my strength came from within. While Madam Gold controlled much of my life, education and the small acts of kindness from Flora became my anchor. Every day was a struggle, but each small victory reminded me that I could endure, survive, and dream of something better.

Chapter 17

The Night I Fought Back

The Night I Fought Back

When fear became strength and survival mattered most.

The last time I called the police was after an incident at Anchodale House in December 2010. It was Saturday night. Madam Gold had returned home from work in the evening. I had cleaned the entire flat, including the toilets. When she saw water on the floor, she accused me of not cleaning properly. I *explained* that one of the boys had urinated on the toilet floor and wall as usual, but she shouted over me, refusing to listen.

Madam Gold attacked me violently. I stumbled into the bedroom, my heart pounding, but she followed relentlessly and shoved me onto the bed. Her hands clamped around my neck, squeezing the air from my lungs. Panic surged through me as I struggled desperately, gasping for breath, until she finally released me.

Before I could recover, she lunged again, her long fingernails raking my lips and mouth. Blood streamed uncontrollably, burning and metallic, and I felt tears sting my eyes. Pain and fear collided inside me, but I refused to give her the satisfaction of complete submission. I bit her hand and pushed her away, though her fists rained down until I could no longer cry out.

She loomed over me, her eyes cold, and asked, "You want to go back to Nigeria?"

"Yes... take me back to my family," I whispered, my voice trembling but filled with longing for safety.

"Get up and pack your things. I'm taking you back tomorrow morning," she snapped. But even as I tried to obey, she struck me again.

"How dare you? After all I have done for you!" she yelled, her rage echoing through the room. She began to rain curses on my parents and anyone connected to me.

Then she grabbed my keys and my phone from the table, locking me inside with nothing but fear and bloodied lips, swollen eyes, bruises on my face and my neck. My whole body ached so much, thinking I had sustained broken bones. That night, I lay awake, heart racing, mind spinning, unable to sleep. Every shadow in the room felt alive, every creak of the floorboards a threat. I felt small, helpless—but deep inside, a quiet ember of determination began to grow.

That Sunday morning, Madam Gold unlocked the bedroom door, placed my keys and phone back in my hands, and left for church with Larry. I remained behind, caring for Joel and Paige, her friend who had just given birth. Despite the pain still throbbing in my neck and the sting in my bleeding mouth, I forced myself into routine—feeding the baby, tidying the flat, and sorting laundry.

While folding clothes at the laundry room, I finally called Flora and poured out everything that had happened. Her voice trembled with compassion. "I'm so sorry you're going through this. Whatever you decide to do, I am here for you," she said. Her words wrapped around me like a blanket, and in that moment, I knew—I could not survive another night in that house. Enough was enough. I said to myself, It will not end like the one previously.

When I returned home from Laundrette, I asked Paige to keep an eye on Joel while I stepped aside. My hands trembled as I dialled Flora once more. Her voice was steady but urgent: *"If you've truly had enough, call for help now."*

That was the push I needed. I looked around the flat, the walls that had witnessed my tears and silence for years, and I knew it was time. I grabbed a Sainsbury's bag, stuffing it with my schoolbooks and a few clothes—just enough to remind myself of who I still was, a Year 11 student preparing for her GCSEs, and not just Madam Gold's housegirl.

Within minutes, the police arrived. Their presence felt unreal—like a lifeline I had only dared to imagine. They took me with them, leaving Joel safely in Paige's care.

I remember how little he was. Just three years old at the time. He clung tightly to me until he was finally distracted with a toy and a pack of crisps.

In that moment, it hit me—he was barely a month old when I first started living with them, and now he was already three. I looked at him with pity as tears rolled down my cheeks. He was more attached to me than to his own mother.

Leaving him behind was one of the hardest things I had to do. But I had no choice.

As I looked at Joel that evening, he trailed behind me, his small footsteps padding across the floor as I packed my things. His eyes searched mine, curious, trusting, unaware. I looked at him with pity, with love so fierce it ached, and I pulled him into my arms. His breath was soft, steady — unaware, unbothered. Safe. Just the way I needed him to be. I didn't know if I'd ever see him again.

Leaving him behind shattered something inside me. Not all wounds bleed. Some just sit inside you, quietly breaking things.

But I had no choice. I had no other way.

Staying would've meant danger — not just for me, but eventually for him, too.

People I'd trusted had turned out to be poison in disguise. And I couldn't let that poison touch him.

He'll be safe...cradled in the warmth of his mother's love, surrounded by everything I can no longer give.

She stirred in the next room, unaware I was still standing there, watching — memorizing. I didn't say goodbye. What would I even say? That I was sorry? That I wished I'd been more, done better? Words felt small against the weight of everything I was leaving behind.

But as for me — staying here would've meant losing more than my freedom. It would've meant losing myself. I'd lose the pieces of myself I still had left.

So I turned. Slowly. Quietly. I walked away — not because I wanted to, but because I had to. Because loving someone sometimes means leaving, even when it tears you apart.

I kissed him gently on the forehead and waved goodbye.

I walked out of that door and didn't look back. I remember the date clearly — it was Sunday evening, December 5th, 2010.

I didn't know what waited ahead, but I knew I couldn't stay. Looking back I know God was on my side. He had it all planned out.

At the station, the officers asked if I had anywhere safe to go. I whispered Flora's name, clinging to the one person who had shown me kindness. Before taking me to her house, they first drove me to the hospital. A doctor examined my neck and head, documenting the bruises and the swelling—silent evidence of what I had endured.

Two officers then went ahead to Flora's home, checking the situation before finally bringing me there. For the first time in years, I felt a small flicker of safety—delivered into the hands of strangers who, for once, chose to protect me.

I didn't return to school the next day. The doctor had advised me to rest, but truthfully, I couldn't have faced the classroom even if I tried. My body ached, and my spirit felt fragile.

A few days later, a social worker named Tao came to Flora's house. She was gentle and calm, and her presence carried a quiet reassurance I hadn't known before. Flora told her I could stay as long as I wanted, and for the first time, I believed I might finally have a place where I was wanted.

When Tao accompanied me to the police station for an interview, the officers videotaped everything. I told them about Madam Gold's endless chores, the shouting, the beatings—but I kept the darkest truth locked inside. I didn't admit that she wasn't my stepmother. Fear had chained my tongue. She had warned me countless times: "If you ever tell anyone I'm not your stepmother, I will kill you. I'll bring trouble to your family too."

So, when the police asked who she was to me, I repeated the story Madam Gold had forced into my mouth since the very beginning—that my mother had died when I was young, that my father had gone to London, and that his second wife had taken me in as her step-daughter. It was a lie I had told at school, to social workers, even to myself. And yet, behind the lies, my heart screamed for someone to see the truth.

The holidays came quietly, without warmth or celebration. Between Christmas and New Year, Tao helped me collect my schoolbooks and bag from Madam Gold's house. I was preparing for my GCSEs, and I needed those books more than anything. They were my one bridge to a future that might free me from the shadows of my past.

Chapter 18

The Voice That Found Me

The Question of Identity

In the New Year, I met with another social worker. During our conversation, I explained how I had seen Larry's Dad and knew, without doubt, that he wasn't my father. It wasn't only his denial—I could feel it in my heart. Blood does not lie.

When the social worker heard this, she looked at me with a softness that nearly made me cry. She said I shouldn't have to carry the surname of a man who isn't my father in any way. For a fleeting moment, the thought of shedding that name felt like shedding a chain. But then, just as quickly, she was gone from my life. I never saw her again.

In the New Year, another social worker sat with me to discuss my wishes. Among them was something that weighed heavily on my heart—I wanted to speak to my mother. I had not heard her voice, not even once, since the day I was taken to live with Madam Gold. The silence between us had become unbearable, like a missing piece of myself.
For years, I had carried questions with no answers. Was she safe? Did she think of me? Did she believe I had forgotten her? Deep inside, I longed for the truth, for a chance to hear her voice and reclaim the part of me that Madam Gold's lies had tried to erase.

The Shadows of Fear Persist.

In March 2011, Hackney Social Services assigned a social worker to visit me. But just days before her arrival, Madam Gold had phoned Flora, her voice dripping with menace. She threatened Flora and her husband for taking me away, and promising she would "show deal with them."

Her words hung over me like a dark cloud, a reminder that fear had never truly left my side. Even with help arriving, I felt the weight of her threats pressing down, the long shadow of her control stretching far beyond the walls of Anchodale House.

Flora held me gently, her presence a quiet anchor amidst the storm of my fear. She encouraged me, softly but firmly, to tell the social worker everything. For the first time, I let the truth spill out.

Finally, the heavy weight of silence lifted, just a little, as the truth was laid bare.

She also guided me on how to contact Clem, ensuring that my story could be fully supported and verified.

For the first time in years, a small spark of hope flickered inside me. There was a path forward, however uncertain, that promised truth, safety, and the chance to reclaim the life Madam Gold had tried to steal.

I had kept a diary filled with telephone numbers, all written down at Madam Gold's insistence—but none had names beside them. Flora suggested we go through each number until we found him, or someone who could point us in the right direction. She bought a phone card, and I began dialling, my heart hammering with every unfamiliar voice.

Each time a voice didn't ring a bell, I hung up and moved to the next number. It was painstaking, but determination pushed me forward—and it didn't take long to find him.

When I finally spoke to Clem, his shock was immediate. He had no idea what had happened to me over the years. His first question was simple, but filled with concern: "Are you safe?" Then he asked about the strange message from Madam Gold—claiming "Rose had called the police". and instructing him to say I was her step-daughter. Clem reminded her that she hadn't reached out to him in three years, and refused to help. Their argument ended abruptly with her hanging up. Instead, Clem promised to go to the village, find my mother, and bring her a phone so I could finally hear her voice.

That evening, Clem called again from the village and gave me my mother's number. When she called back, my chest tightened with emotion. Hearing her voice after so many years was overwhelming—her joy mirrored my own. I told her where I was, but she didn't fully understand. When she said she would take the bus to see me, I had to tell her it was too far. Even so, the connection, even over the phone, was everything I had longed for, a lifeline to the part of myself that had been missing for far too long.

Rebuilding Connection.

Over the following days, I spoke to my mother whenever we could manage it. Each conversation was a lifeline, a reminder of who I truly was beyond the confines of Madam Gold's house. Her voice carried warmth, love, and reassurance—the very things I had been starved of for so long.

Through those calls, I began to feel pieces of myself returning. I shared stories of school, of the small victories and daily struggles, and she listened with care, asking questions and offering guidance. Even from afar, her presence grounded me.

Flora remained my steadfast support during this time, helping coordinate calls and making sure I felt safe. Together, we slowly navigated the logistics of reconnecting, piecing together a relationship that had been severed for far too long.

Although the distance remained, hearing my mother's voice, feeling her concern and love, ignited a sense of hope I hadn't felt in years. For the first time, I sensed that there might be a future where I could be free, supported, and truly myself.

Finally, my mother sent my baptismal and birth certificates to me through DHL. Holding those documents in my hands felt like reclaiming a piece of myself that had been lost for years—a tangible proof of who I truly was.

Holding my mother's voice in my heart and her documents in my hands, I felt a sense of belonging I had longed for my entire life. After years of fear, lies, and isolation, I finally began to reclaim not just my identity, but also my hope, my family, and a future where I could truly be myself.

Chapter 19

A Valley Encounter

The valley wasn't just another spot on the map; it was a moment that changed everything. It was a place where my past, my uncertainties, and a faint but real hope for what lay ahead all came together. I remember that day so vividly—it almost feels like the valley itself left a mark on my soul. I stood there early in the morning, surrounded by thick mist that clung to my skin and sank deep into my bones. Every step felt heavier, as if the ground were testing my strength. My heart pounded—not just with fear, but with a strange mix of nerves and hope I couldn't yet name.

I'd heard stories about valleys—how they can be dangerous, how they can also be places of breakthrough. But nothing prepared me for what I was about to experience on a deeper, more spiritual level. The silence was almost complete, broken only by distant birds and the soft rustle of leaves. It felt like the whole world was holding its breath, waiting for something extraordinary to happen.

As I walked further in, memories from my past came rushing back with each step—the pain of being trafficked, the faces of those who hurt me, the broken promises, and the weight of betrayal and loss that pressed heavily on my chest. I felt small, invisible—just a shadow of the person I once hoped to become.

In that moment of deep vulnerability, I dropped to my knees. Tears streamed down my cheeks, hot and relentless. I cried out—not just with my voice, but with everything in me. I begged God for help, for a sign that I wasn't alone in this empty, sacred place.

My words echoed through the valley, fading into the vast stillness around me.

Within seconds, one of my favourite quotes from years ago flashed through my mind:

"He that has brought you this far will complete what He started."

Then, in the quiet, I sensed something—like a presence I had never felt before. The air around me seemed to shift, filled with a warmth and light I couldn't explain. I couldn't see it with my eyes, but I felt it deep within my spirit. A calmness, a deep and lasting peace, settled over me. The fear that had gripped my heart began to loosen.

At first, I wondered if I was just imagining things. But as I sat there, I began to notice a gentle whisper—something I couldn't hear with my ears but could feel clearly in my heart. It was a voice speaking of love, forgiveness, and purpose.

"You must let all hurt go," the voice whispered.

It reassured me that my pain wasn't pointless—that every tear I had shed was seen, heard, and counted. That presence felt like it was holding me, as if I were being cradled by unseen hands.

In that moment, I became convinced I was not alone after all. I remembered my name: **Chinasa**—*"God answers."* And in that valley, I knew without a doubt: God was speaking directly to me.
It felt as though my prayers had finally been answered.

The shame and guilt I had carried for years began to fade, replaced by a deep sense of worth and belonging. I saw visions—memories from my childhood, moments of happiness and laughter—reminders that I was more than my hurts, more than my low self-worth. I glimpsed a future filled with hope, a life built on faith and strength.

This spiritual experience wasn't like something you see in movies—there were no dramatic scenes. But it was powerful, and it was real. It felt as though that valley had become holy ground, a place where heaven and earth met. That encounter changed me.

I got up with a new sense of purpose. The valley—once a symbol of despair—had become a place of hope. I realised my story wasn't just about surviving; it was about overcoming. That spiritual moment gave me the courage to forgive—both the people who hurt me, and myself.

Emotionally lighter, almost as if a heavy weight had been lifted from my shoulders. I began to see things differently. The worries and sadness that had once weighed me down started to loosen their grip. Spiritually, I became aware—maybe for the first time—of God's love and presence. It was like I was seeing with new eyes, no longer defined by my past mistakes, but by the promises God had made to me.

I left that valley with a fresh sense of faith. Prayer was no longer something I did out of habit; it became my lifeline, my way of staying connected to the Source. I learned to trust in what I couldn't see—to believe that even in the darkest times, light could still break through.

That experience in the valley wasn't just a spiritual moment—it felt like I was being reborn.

As I share this part of my story, I hope others going through their own valleys know they're not alone. Hard times aren't easy, but they're often the very place where we meet God in a special way. It's where we're stripped of pretence and invited to face our deepest fears—and our greatest hopes.

If you're in a valley right now, know this: that's not how your story ends. There is hope, even when everything looks hopeless. Healing is possible, even when wounds feel like they'll never close. My time in the valley showed me that God listens, that faith combined with action can do amazing things, and that pain can become a source of strength. Looking back, I see that valley as a gift—something I didn't ask for but truly needed to bring me to where God wants me to be. It's where I discovered how deep God's love really is.

The experience wasn't about visions or miracles, but about the quiet reassurance that I am seen, known, and loved. That emotional impact stays with me still. I'm more compassionate, more understanding of what others are going through. I've learned to listen for hope's faint whispers, even amid chaos.

That valley experience began my journey toward healing—a journey I continue with every step I take. The valley didn't erase my struggles overnight, but it gave me the tools to handle them better. I learned to lean on my faith, to ask for support from those who care, and to use my story to encourage others.

It gave me a powerful testimony—a story of redemption I now share proudly.

I am no longer defined by what happened to me, but by what God has done within me. That valley moment was a crossroads of pain and grace. It's a chapter I will always mark as shaping the woman I am becoming.

The valley was both a challenge and a triumph. It was where I met God in my deepest despair and found the courage to move forward. The spiritual and emotional lessons I learned there are hard to put into words.

When everything in my life changed, that moment was the turning point. As you read this, I pray you find your own valley moment. May you experience a peace beyond understanding, a love that heals all wounds, and a faith that guides you from darkness into light. The valley isn't the end—it's just the start of a new chapter filled with hope, healing, and purpose.

Chapter 20

Secrets and Confidants

The moment I experienced in the valley was a huge turning point. It changed my outlook on so many levels—emotionally, spiritually, and even socially. It was deeply personal, something that truly shaped who I am now.

At the same time, I couldn't talk about it openly with just anyone. This part of my life was delicate—I had to find the right balance between sharing my spiritual awakening and keeping it as a sacred secret. I also depended on one close friend who became my biggest supporter—her name is Flora.

Yet, inside me, there was a tension: How do I stay true to my personal needs while meeting the expectations of family and my church community?

After the valley experience, I felt hopeful and more connected to my faith. Still, I was hesitant to tell others what I had gone through. I wanted it to remain a secret at all costs. Even when people asked about my family, I responded in a way that gave away no clues. I suspected that everything and everyone might betray me at the first opportunity.

It was such a personal and powerful moment, yet I feared exposing myself to judgment or misunderstandings. I worried people might dismiss my experience or see it as something minor. There were several reasons I kept quiet. For one, the experience was deeply emotional and supernatural—it's not something easy to explain or convey to others.

I feared my family and church community might be judgmental or even disapprove. I was part of the African church community, where certain events are considered normal and expected. Growing up in a culture that values conformity, new spiritual experiences that challenge the norms are often met with suspicion. I just knew I'd face resistance if I spoke openly about what I had been through. In fact, I had so many questions myself that, at one point, I wondered what the point of opening up even was.

Second, my past trauma made me extremely cautious about trusting people—I had zero trust. I saw everyone as a potential betrayal. Having been through trafficking and betrayal, I learned the hard way that not everyone would treat my truth with care. The moment I experienced in the valley was like a fragile seed of healing, and I knew I had to protect it from harsh or unknowing reactions that might damage it. I was still trying to understand what had really happened myself. Sometimes, I wonder how everything happened so fast. The emotions and spiritual feelings I experienced were so intense that I needed time to process everything before I could feel comfortable sharing it.

It felt like a sacred moment that deserved respect and reflection—not something to be hurried or explained right away. Even though I kept quiet at first, I knew I couldn't carry this burden alone. I needed trustworthy people—those who could listen without judgment, support me in my healing, and honour the special nature of what I had experienced.

Slowly, I began opening up to a few close friends—my confidants. One of these was Flora, a woman I mentioned earlier. I met her while taking Madam Gold's children to school. Madam Gold was the woman who trafficked me into the United Kingdom.

Over time, Flora and I bonded deeply. There was a connection between us—physical, spiritual, and emotional. We even shared the same birthday month.

The first question she always asked was, "Are you okay?" Somehow, she knew things weren't alright with me.

When I finally told her about my experience in the valley, she was surprised—but responded with kindness and encouragement. She didn't dismiss what I felt or try to explain it away. Instead, she acknowledged my experience as real and told me to hold onto the peace and purpose it had brought me. She reminded me that everything happens for a reason, even if I couldn't fully comprehend it then.

Flora was empathetic, understanding, and supportive—it felt like we had known each other for years. Our relationship grew stronger with every meeting. She prayed for me every day.

As days turned to months, and months into years, Flora became the one person I could pour my heart out to. She knew everything about me and became my trusted confidant. She fought for me and sought help in many ways. When I finally escaped Madam Gold, Flora and her husband welcomed me into their home, offering me a safe place to heal.

Another person I trusted deeply was my husband. Our relationship was built on trust and support, so I felt safe sharing my deepest fears and hopes with him. He listened carefully and prayed with me daily, providing strength and reassurance with every step and decision I took. His faith and understanding made me feel less alone and more grounded in my new reality.

I also spoke with a mentor before deciding to pursue nursing as a career. With her years of teaching and experience, she helped prepare me for what lay ahead. Her wisdom guided me in balancing my personal journey with the expectations of both my church community and family.

While living with Flora, I joined the Africans Unite Against Child Abuse (AFRUCA) organisation. As a charitable organisation dedicated to supporting those with lived experience of trafficking, AFRUCA became a turning point for me. I was deeply shocked to meet so many other women, young girls, and men with stories painfully similar to mine. Knowing I wasn't alone brought a mix of comfort and sorrow—comfort in shared understanding, and sorrow for how widespread our pain really was. While these people accepted my story, I couldn't ignore the tension it caused with the wider expectations of my family and church.

Coming from an Igbo cultural and Christian background, spiritual experiences are often interpreted through specific traditions and doctrines. When someone shares something deeply personal especially if it doesn't fit into those established norms—it's often met with suspicion or even quiet rejection.

My family has always been deeply rooted in both cultural and religious values. Privacy was seen as a strength. They believed in keeping personal struggles to themselves and maintaining the family's reputation at all costs. I was expected to stay strong in silence, to carry whatever burden came my way without letting it show. Sharing the supernatural experience had felt risky. It might be seen as attention-seeking, delusional, or even unstable. I feared they wouldn't understand—it could cause worry, or worse, distance. So I chose not to tell them everything. Within my church community, too, there was an unspoken pressure to present a polished image of faith—one that left little room for questions, struggles, or unusual spiritual experiences.

It was about showing up regularly, doing good works, and following the doctrines—rather than speaking openly about personal spiritual moments.

The encounter I had in the valley was deeply personal and mystical. It didn't fit into the usual mold. I feared that sharing it might create distance between me and others—or invite judgment I wasn't ready to face. So, I learned to compartmentalise my experience. I stayed active in the church—singing in the choir, praying, volunteering—while keeping the deeper parts of my spiritual journey tucked quietly inside. It became a careful balancing act: honouring what I knew to be true for me, while respecting the emotional and cultural boundaries of those I loved.

Keeping the valley encounter a secret was both difficult and, in some ways, freeing.

On one hand, it protected me from judgment and preserved the sacredness of the experience. It allowed me to nurture my faith privately and grow spiritually—without external pressure or interference. But on the other hand, silence could be lonely. There were moments when I longed to share the full story, to be seen, understood, and accepted completely. Keeping it to myself created a quiet distance between me and others who hadn't walked the same path. That loneliness sometimes weighed heavily.

Still, the struggle taught me valuable lessons—about trust, discernment, and what it truly means to be part of a spiritual community. I learned that not everyone is ready to hear certain truths. And that's okay.

I began to honour my own pace and boundaries, choosing to open up only to those who could truly walk with me and support my journey.

As my faith deepened and my confidence grew, I slowly started sharing more of my story. I found strength in my testimony—speaking about God's faithfulness and the power of prayer. What once felt too sacred to speak about became a source of encouragement for others navigating their own valleys.

The people I trusted became my allies, helping me navigate the delicate balance between family expectations, church culture, and my personal spiritual growth. Together, we built a small circle of trust—a space where healing and progress could happen naturally. That community became my safe haven, a place where my spiritual journey was not only respected but also celebrated.

After that valley encounter, I found myself doing a lot of inner work while carefully navigating my social world. I chose very intentionally who to share my experience with, trying to strike a balance between seeking support and respecting the cultural and religious beliefs around me.

The friends I opened up to became truly priceless—offering love, understanding, and encouragement when I needed it most. This part of my story is a reminder that healing isn't always loud or public. Sometimes, it's a quiet, sacred process that unfolds in private. It takes courage to remain true to yourself—even in silence. I've been blessed to find people who held my truth with care. As I move forward, I carry with me the lessons I've learned about trust, discretion, and the power of safe spaces. Some truths are meant to be shared. Others are meant to be kept sacred. But all of them, I now know, are held in the light of God's endless love.

Chapter 21

Growing Pains

Growth is rarely a direct route. Instead, it is a zigzag road, with twists and turns, dead ends and detours, and victories small and large. Despite the valley experience, I was filled with hope and purpose, but the road ahead was not an easy one to travel. The trauma that followed, the demands of family and community, the struggle to create my own identity all came together to challenge me.

This chapter is about the pains and lessons learned growing up—at home and within the community in London.

Home was my initial school and my initial battlefield. I was the first child of my parents, so I had expectations that at times felt too much for my little shoulders. My mother, a pillar of strength and endurance, worked day and night to support us. She was also a virtuoso at creating much from little, transforming plain foods into banquets and a humble house into home. But her love was best shown in hard work instead of words or kisses.

As I grew up, I found myself stuck between gratitude and yearning. I respected my mother's strength, yet I yearned for her nurturing. Some days I wish she would stop and sit with me and listen to my nightmares and aspirations. But she was always on the move—washing, cooking, hauling water, or taking care of my younger siblings. I learned from a young age that love could be sacrificial and quiet, but a piece of me still longed for expressing affection openly.

My father, "Nna Unoego," was a popular man in our community. His pride in me was evident, but his hopes were great. He expected me to be an example to my siblings and to maintain the family's dignity. When he died in 2018, I felt my burden of his legacy even more heavily. I wanted to make him proud, but I also wrestled with feeling like I was not perfect.

And as I grew up, I understood that my parents' habits were a response to their own struggles and backgrounds. My mother's hard exterior was her shield, strengthened by years of adversity. My father's pride was his attempt at affection. To appreciate this made me forgive them for their flaws and respect them for their sacrifices. And it taught me the value of declaring love in full view—a lesson I try to enact with my children.

If home was my initial battleground, the village was my proving ground. In my village, there were no strangers. My name—Unoego—had a history and a set of expectations. Being "Nna Unoego's daughter" meant I was observed, critiqued, and occasionally envied. The village was warm in its support, but it was also merciless.

Growing up, I adored the life in the compound—the communal meals, the market days, the shouts of laughter in the evenings. But as I matured, I grew more conscious of the eyes of the community. They gossiped. They recollected it all—who flunked a test, who got into trouble, who did well. I was under the pressure to perform at all times, to never shame my people.

This scrutiny increased after my encounter with trafficking and my escape. Some viewed me with sympathy; others with suspicion. Rumors were spread, and whispers were made. Some envied me, others perceived me as a victim, some as someone who had invited trouble upon herself. It hurt to know that not everyone could sympathize and accept my experience.

But the community also provided glimpses of grace. There were neighbors who showed me kindness, friends who did not leave me, and elders who prayed for me. These were moments that reminded me community had the power to heal as much as it did to hurt. I learned to identify my people in the greater crowd—those who did not just accept me for what they heard, but those who accepted me for who I am.

School was my passport to a better future, yet it was also something I worried about. I was adamant to succeed, to convince myself and everyone else that there was more to me than my background. But the journey wasn't easy.

There were topics I had difficulty with, instructors who questioned my abilities, tests I flunked. I recall the bitter taste of disappointment when I did not place at the head of the class, the embarrassment of returning home with a dreadful report card. My mum were dismayed, and I felt as though I had disappointed them.

But failure taught me. Every failure compelled me to stand face-to-face with my weaknesses and to learn to be resilient. I learned to seek assistance, to work more diligently, and to have faith in myself even when others lacked faith in me. And eventually, I learned that failure wasn't the end but rather a stepping stone to progress.

One of the most difficult lessons was how to utilise my voice. In my culture, children—particularly girls—were taught to be seen, not heard. Speaking out against elders or discussing personal issues was discouraged.

But since my experience in the valley, I have felt a renewed sense of purpose. I wanted to tell my story, to inspire others, and to stand up for victims of trafficking. I was frightened at first. What if others judged me? What if they did not listen to me? What if my story brought shame to my family?

The first time I publicly shared my experience, my hands shook and my voice quivered. But when I spoke, I could see the effects of what I was saying on others. People listened, some crying tears. I knew then that my story had strength—not only to heal me, but to give hope to others.

It was not always easy to speak out. There were instances when I was criticised or misunderstood. People accused me of being an attention-seeker; others doubted my intentions. The majority believed I was seeking pity. But I learned to be steadfast in my truth. I knew I could not satisfy everyone, and it was fine. My duty was to remain true to myself and to speak out for good because lives have been touched.

My faith was as much a source of strength as it was a source of struggle. I was closer to God than I ever had been after my supernatural encounter in the valley. Prayer was my haven. I became a praise addict. I praised and worshipped God at every given time. They were my survival line. But faith did not remove my doubts and struggles.

There were times when I questioned God—why had I endured so much suffering? Why did healing linger on and on? Why did some of my prayers go unanswered? There were evenings when the fear and anxiety came back, when old wounds opened up once more.

But out of these struggles, faith grew in me. I learned that faith was not a lack of doubt, but courage to trust God in the midst of the unknown. The faith I had was believing in the things I prayed to become my reality. I found that God's presence was not always dramatic, but sometimes quiet and consistent—a soft and gentle whisper and nudging in the storms. I realised this is the work of the Holy Spirit – this is how he led me.

I also learned to rely on my church family, though it was not perfect. Singing in the choir, ministering to others, and fellowship helped me keep my feet planted. I had mentors who directed me, friends who prayed with me, and a feeling of belonging that carried me through.

Becoming a mother was both a gift and a new round of challenges. My children became my inspiration to heal and become stronger. I wanted to provide them with the love and security I often did not have. But motherhood also opened my vulnerabilities. I began to put myself in my mother's shoes. Many times, I wonder how she was able to raise us with so little.

There were times when I was at my wit's end—balancing work, school, and parenting. There were times when I erupted in anger or felt incompetent. I was afraid of doing what my parents had done, being absent too much, of failing my kids. I regretted being away from my kids. There was mummy guilt, but I reassured myself I will do my very best for my children.

But motherhood showed me how to be kind to myself. I realised that perfection was not feasible, but presence was strength. I prioritised spending quality time with my children—to eat, play, and pray together. I apologised when I erred and celebrated small wins.

Motherhood also strengthened my spirituality. I felt God's grace in my children's laughter, in their hugs and in their questions. They taught me about the necessity of joy, curiosity, and unconditional love.

A career in nursing was a dream come true, but it had its own growing pains. Nursing is physically, emotionally, and mentally demanding. There were long shifts, challenging patients, and times of self-doubt.

I recall my initial days as a staff nurse in London. The hospital was busy, and the standards were high. I erred—giving the wrong drug, overlooking crucial information, and having difficulty communicating with colleagues from diverse backgrounds. Every mistake was like a failure, a validation of my worst fears.

But I would not give up. I asked for feedback, learned from my mistakes, and slowly built my confidence. I found the satisfaction of caring for others, of making a difference in one's life. Nursing taught me compassion, strength, and the value of ongoing learning.

Subsequently, when I was given the chance to train as a Health Visitor, I encountered new challenges. The training was rigorous, the workload substantial. Juggling work, study, and family life was draining. There were evenings when I wept with exhaustion, mornings when I questioned my competence, and days I questioned myself non-stop.

But every obstacle became a lesson. I learned to ask for help, to put boundaries in place, and to take care of myself. I learned that growth is oftentimes through struggle, and that each failure is a chance to learn.

One of the greatest lessons I have learned along the way is how to forgive—others and myself. The hurt of the past, the things I did wrong, the individuals that hurt me—each left a scar. For years, I nursed anger and resentment, thinking that forgiveness was about letting them off the hook for what had been done.

But I learned that forgiveness is not about forgetting or condoning, but about freeing myself from the grip of the past. It is about choosing to heal, to move forward, to reclaim my power. Forgiving myself was even harder. I had to let go of the guilt and shame, to accept that I was worthy of love and happiness.

There were times when I faltered—when fear or anger directed my actions, when I damaged the people I loved, when I did not live up to my own ideals. But every failure was an occasion to expand, to learn, and to attempt again.

As I reflect on my path, I noticed how every struggle, every failure, and every lesson molded me. I'm not the same quivering girl who questioned her value. I am a woman who has walked through darkness and emerged into light, who has fallen and got up, and who has learned to love her narrative.

Maturity, I have come to understand, is not a matter of knowing it all, but of being open to asking the tough questions. It is being able to accept imperfection, pursue growth, and give grace to oneself and others. It is being strong in weakness and finding purpose in suffering.

I am still learning, still growing. Some days I am strong and capable, some days I am not. But I am dedicated to the process—to being the best version of myself, for my family, my community, and myself.

Growing pains are painful, yes, but they are a blessing too. They remind us that we exist, that we are evolving, that we are growing. My journey has not been easy, but it has been worth it. It has been peppered with struggle and victory, despair and hope. Each trial has been an opportunity to learn something worthwhile—about myself, about people, about life.

As I grow on, I appreciate the aches that have molded me. They have made me strong, understanding, and experienced. They have provided me with a narrative worth recounting—a narrative of endurance, trust, and change.

To anyone reading this who is experiencing their own growing pains, I want you to know that you're not alone. Growth is difficult, but it's also gorgeous. Hold on tight to the journey, learn from every fall, and have faith that, with time, you'll come out stronger, wiser, and more fully yourself.

Chapter 22

Trials and Triumphs

The most significant and defining crisis in my life was being a victim of child trafficking. This was not a distant tragedy or a story I heard from someone else, but a personal and harrowing experience that shaped the very core of my being. Trafficking, as I have come to know intimately, is more real and devastating than most people can imagine. It is a trauma that leaves deep scars—physically, emotionally, psychologically, mentally and spiritually. It affects a person in ways one cannot fully explain. Some that I know hardly recover from the ordeal.

As a child, I was taken from the familiarity of my home and thrust into an environment of fear, uncertainty, and exploitation. The sense of helplessness was overwhelming. I was young, vulnerable, and unable to comprehend why such evil existed in the world. Every day was a battle for survival, and every night was haunted by nightmares of what I had endured. The trauma manifested in many ways—post-traumatic stress disorder (PTSD), sleep disturbances, depression, anxiety, and a profound sense of shame and distrust.

Yet, even in the darkest moments, a small spark of hope remained. My faith became both a shield and a lifeline. I clung to praise and worship, often when words failed me during prayer, and only tears were all that was left. I believed, sometimes desperately, that God saw me, that He had not abandoned me, and that I would be free one day. If I'm asked, Faith is believing in the unseen reality—the sixth sense that assures your hope and expectation will become a reality someday. Even when it looked impossible in every way.

The journey out of trafficking was not easy. It required courage to seek help, even when fear tried to silence me. I had to confront not only my trafficker but also the doubts within myself. Was I worthy of freedom? Could I ever be whole again? Each step toward escape was taken in fear, but also in faith. "Now faith is confidence in what we hope for and assurance about what we do not see". Hebrews 11:1 (NIV). Faith and resilience worked hand in hand at the time, and have always done. It was faith that kept me resilient. I learned that resilience is not the absence of fear, but the decision to keep moving forward despite it.

With time, support, and unwavering faith in God's word, I found my way out. The scars remained, but they became reminders of what I had survived, not what defined me. Healing was a gradual process. I had to relearn how to trust, how to sleep without nightmares, and how to see myself not as a victim, but as a survivor. My faith played a central role in this transformation. I poured my pain into prayer, into singing, and into helping others who were still trapped in their own darkness.

Resilience is not something you are born with; it is forged in the fires of adversity. My experience with trafficking taught me that resilience is the ability to bend without breaking, to endure hardship and emerge stronger. It is the quiet strength that allows you to keep going when everything inside you wants to give up.

I found resilience in the small victories—each day I survived, each night I found a moment of peace, each time I reached out for help. I learned to celebrate progress, no matter how slow and small. I discovered that sharing my story was not just cathartic for me, but also a source of healing and hope for others. My pain became my purpose, and my survival became a testimony to the power of faith and perseverance.

Throughout my ordeal, faith in God's words was my anchor. It was not a passive belief, but an active force that propelled me forward. I believed that God had a plan for my life, even when I could not see it. I trusted that my suffering was not in vain and that one day, I would use my experience to help others.

Prayer became my refuge. When I could not find the words, I sang most of the time. Music was a form of worship and a way to connect with God when my spirit was too broken to speak. I surrounded myself with scriptures and songs that reminded me of God's promises. "A cheerful heart is a good medicine, but a broken spirit saps a person's strength" (Proverbs 17:22)—these words became a mantra, a reminder to seek joy even in pain.

Escaping trafficking was only the beginning. The true triumph was reclaiming my life and finding purpose in my pain. I pursued my education, determined to build a future that was not defined by my past. I completed my Bachelor of Science in Adult Nursing at the University of Hertfordshire, even taking a year out to have my first child and returning to finish my degree.

Many doubted that I could succeed, but I proved them wrong through hard work and God's help. This brings me to say that you can achieve whatever you put your mind to. Becoming a nurse was more than a career—it was a calling. I wanted to provide compassionate care to others, to be a source of comfort and hope as others had been to me.

Nursing allowed me to heal not only myself but also those around me.

My family became my greatest source of joy. My children, my husband, and the simple moments we shared were treasures I refused to take for granted. I learned to prioritize time with them, to laugh, to cook, and to create memories that would outshine the darkness of my past. As my family grew, I sensed a need for a change - achieving a work-life balance became a need that would benefit us. Five years after my Degree, I went back to City of London University. This is where I obtained a graduate Diploma award, enabling me to work as a Specialist Community Public Health Nurse - a health visitor. I consider myself fortunate to have met the needs of newborn babies, their families and local communities through the Healthy Child Programme legal framework. It's indeed life-changing to see that a difference is made in every little way each day.

My journey inspired me to become an advocate for others who have suffered similar fates. I wrote this book not only as a legacy for my children and grandchildren, but also as a beacon of hope for anyone trapped in the cycle of trauma and despair. I want my story to empower, encourage and educate others to believe that escape is possible, that healing is real, and that faith in God's words can move mountains.

I thank God for the strength to have pursued further education and become a Specialist Community Public Health nurse. This role allowed me to balance my career and family life while continuing to serve my community. I am grateful for the opportunities I have had and the ability to make the most of them.

Today, I am not just a survivor—I am a testament to the power of resilience, God's protection, and faith. My journey through the valley of trafficking and trauma has taught me that no crisis is insurmountable when you hold onto hope. I have learned to see myself not as a victim, but as a victor. My scars are not a source of shame, but a badge of honour.

To anyone facing their own trials, I say: if I could overcome, so can you! Let your faith in God be your guide, your resilience your shield, and your story your legacy. Trials may come, but triumph is possible for those who refuse to give up.

Chapter 23

Miracles and Meaning

When I look back over the tapestry of my life, I see not just the hardship and pain, but also the golden threads of miracles—moments of divine intervention, unexplained events, and blessings that arrived when hope seemed lost. These moments have strengthened my faith, worldview, and the core of who I am, and who I am becoming. They are the reason I believe deeply in the power of prayer, the mystery of God's timing, and the reality that we are never truly alone, even in our darkest hours. I have seen too many to believe there are no accidents; every event and incident were predestined by the one who created us, and their occurrences were for a purpose. They are a manifestation of what was written in the pages of our lives before our existence. "You saw me before I was born. Every day of my life was recorded in your book. Every moment was laid out before a single day had passed" – Psalm 139: 16 (NLT).

Growing up in Anambra State, in a family where faith was woven into the fabric of our daily lives, I learned early to look for the hand of God in small things. My mother, a woman of tireless energy and unwavering faith, would often pause in the middle of her chores to whisper a prayer and give thanks to God for sending forth rain to water the farm. She believed, as I do now, that every blessing—no matter how small—was a sign of God's mercy, his love and faithfulness. He is always on time, believe me when I say this. I have seen God come through for my family at unexpected times, through mysterious and supernatural ways that cannot be explained or understood most time. God's timing is indeed the best according to his promise to his people.

There were times, especially in my early childhood, when food was scarce and when illness swept through the village. I remember one particular season when the crops failed to yield harvest, my parent - Mum worried over how we would eat. I was too young to understand the full weight of their anxiety, but I remember my mother gathering us together, her voice steady as she prayed for provision. The very next day, a neighbour arrived with a basket overflowing with cassava, corn, okra and vegetables, saying she'd felt compelled to share her harvest with us. My mother wept tears of gratitude. I learned my first lesson in miracles that sometimes, God answers through the hands of other people. Of all the miracles in my life, none is more profound than my escape from trafficking. It is a story I have told before, but one that bears repeating, for it is the clearest evidence I have that God intervenes in the affairs of those who call upon Him.

There were days—long, endless days—when hope seemed like a distant memory. I was trapped, powerless, my spirit battered by fear and uncertainty. Yet, even in those moments, there were signs. A kind word from a stranger, a door left unlocked, a sudden change in routine—each one a thread that, when woven together, became my path to freedom.

I remember the evening I finally escaped. The air was thick with tension, every shadow a threat. I had prayed for deliverance, not knowing how or when it would come. Then, as if guided by an unseen hand, I found myself alone, the usual watchful eyes distracted by a commotion outside. My heart pounded as I slipped through the door, my feet moving almost of their own accord. I made that phone call despite been filled with fear of the unknown. I was almost drowned by fear, having had several unsuccessful attempts in the last years. Though I was afraid, I still decided without looking back. I knew I had to keep trying, even when I don't know what lies ahead on the other side. I became familiar with what this quotation says "It's not how many times you fall that counts, it's how many times you get back up". This quotation kept me going strong. Do you know what, I refused to stop trying. Giving up was not an option as the level of abuse increased by the day. I have had enough. It's either I now or prepare to be buried. The latter has been made known to me countless times.

Looking back, I see that evening as a miracle—not just the escape itself, but the countless small interventions that made it possible. The timing was too perfect, the coincidences too many. I am convinced that God was with me, guiding my steps, shielding me from harm.

Life has a way of surprising us, of placing us in situations where the only explanation is divine intervention. I have experienced this again and again, in ways both dramatic and subtle.

During my university years in the United Kingdom, there were moments when I felt overwhelmed—by studies, by motherhood, by the weight of expectations. There were nights when I sat up late, tears streaming down my face, unsure how I would make it through. Yet, time after time, something would happen to remind me I was not alone. A friend would call just when I needed encouragement. An unexpected financial aid would arrive. A lecturer would grant me an extension without my even asking.

One memory stands out: I was struggling to balance my coursework with caring for my newborn. I prayed for strength, for wisdom, for a sign that I was on the right path. That week, I received a letter from the university offering additional support for student mothers—a program I hadn't even known existed. It felt like a direct answer to my prayer, a reminder that God sees even the needs we cannot articulate.

Even my names—Roseline, Chinasa, Egodi, Unoego—are reminders of miracles and meaning. Chinasa, "God answers," is a daily affirmation that my life is a testimony to answered prayers. Egodi, "there is money," and Unoego, "house of money," speak to the abundance that followed my birth, a year of harvest and blessing for my family. These names are not just labels; they are declarations of faith, reminders that I am known and loved by a God who provides.

There have been times when I doubted my worth, when the trauma of my past threatened to define me. Yet, in those moments, I remembered my names, the stories behind them, and the miracles that accompanied my arrival into this world. They anchored me, reminding me that I am more than my circumstances.

Not all miracles are dramatic. Many are quiet, woven into the fabric of daily life. Waking up each morning healthy, seeing my children's smiles, having food on the table—these are miracles I refuse to take for granted. My work as a nurse has only deepened this awareness. I have seen patients recover against all odds, families reunited, hope restored in the bleakest situations. Each time, I am reminded that life itself is not just a miracle, it's a gift and must be lived to the pleasure of the giver.

There was a patient—a young mother—who arrived in critical condition. The prognosis was grim, but her family prayed, and we did all we could. Against every expectation, she recovered. When she left the hospital, she hugged me and whispered, "God sent you to me." In that moment, I felt the presence of something greater than myself, a reminder that we are often vessels for miracles in the lives of others.

Music has always been a source of spiritual comfort for me. There have been days when I could not find the words to pray, but a song would rise in my heart, lifting me out of despair. Singing in the choir, praising God in songs, has brought me closer to the divine than any sermon ever could.

Laughter, too, is a miracle. In the darkest moments, a well-timed joke or a child's giggle has broken the spell of fear and reminded me that joy is possible, even in suffering. I have learned to cherish these moments, to see them as gifts—evidence that God delights in our happiness.

I have always been intuitive, able to sense things before they happen or to know the right path without proof. Some call it a "sixth sense"; I call it the whisper of the Holy Spirit. There have been times when I felt a nudge to call someone, to take a different route, to pause and pray—and later discovered that these small acts made all the difference.

One night, I dreamed of my father, who had passed away years before. In the dream, he smiled and told me everything would be alright. The next day, I received news that a problem I had been worrying about had resolved itself. Was it coincidence? Perhaps. But I choose to see it as a message, a reminder that those who love us never truly leave.

What do these miracles mean? For me, they are reminders that life is more than random chance. They are evidence of a loving God who cares for us, who intervenes in ways both seen and unseen. They are proof that prayer works—not always in the way we expect, but always in the way we need.

Miracles have taught me humility. They remind me that I am not in control that I must trust in a wisdom greater than my own. They have taught me gratitude, to see every blessing as a gift, every challenge as an opportunity for growth.

Most importantly, they have taught me hope. Even in the darkest moments, I have learned to look for the light, to believe that better days are possible. This hope is not naive; it is forged in the fires of experience, tempered by loss and suffering, but unbroken.

Because of these experiences, I see the world differently. I believe in the power of faith, in the importance of kindness, in the necessity of hope. I believe that every person we meet is fighting a battle we cannot see, and that a single act of compassion can change a life.

I have learned to listen for the quiet voice of God, to trust the nudges and whispers that guide me. I have learned to pray not just for myself, but for others, believing that our stories are intertwined, that my miracle may be the answer to someone else's prayer.

I see suffering not as a punishment, but as a part of the human journey—a place where miracles are born. I have seen too much to ever doubt that God is real, that He cares, and that He is always working for our good, even when we cannot see it.

As I write these words, I am filled with gratitude. My life is not perfect, but it is rich with meaning. The miracles I have experienced are not just for me; they are a legacy I pass on to my children, my grandchildren, and to everyone who reads my story.

I want them to know that miracles are real, that faith is powerful, and that hope is never wasted. I want them to see that even in the darkest night, there are stars. That every prayer is heard, every tear is counted, and every story matters.

Today, I live with expectation. I wake each morning believing that something good is possible, that miracles are waiting to be discovered. I pray, I sing, I laugh, I love—and in all these things, I see the hand of God.

If you are reading this and wondering if miracles still happen, let my story be your answer. They do. Sometimes they come as thunderbolts, sometimes as whispers, sometimes as the quiet, steady presence of love in a world that can be so harsh.

I am a survivor, yes. But more than that, I am a witness—to grace, to mercy, to the miracles that shape our lives and give them meaning.

Chapter 24

Coming of Age

Coming of age is not a single moment, but a series of awakenings—some gentle, some abrupt—that mark the journey from childhood innocence to the complex world of adulthood. As I reflect on my own transition, I see it as a tapestry woven from joy and pain, faith and doubt, triumph and failure. Each thread is a memory, a lesson, a turning point that shaped the woman I am today.

My childhood in Anambra State was, in many ways, idyllic. I was the first child of my mother, a source of pride and joy, and the recipient of names that spoke of abundance, faith, and hope. I grew up surrounded by family, traditions, and the rhythms of village life—market days, communal meals, laughter around the fire and moon dance. My mother's cooking filled our home with warmth, and her songs echoed through the compound, a constant reminder that I was loved until my parent separated and began to live apart.

But innocence is fragile. It is easily shattered by the realities of life—by loss, by separation, divorce, disappointment, by the knowledge that not everyone's heart is as pure as your own. For me, the first cracks appeared as I became aware of the world beyond our village. I saw the struggles of those around me, the sacrifices my parents made, and the unspoken worries that sometimes clouded their faces.

One memory stands out: the day I learned that my father's strength was not infinite. He was a pillar in our community, respected and admired, but I saw him weep when a close friend died unexpectedly. It was the first time I realized that even the strongest people are vulnerable, that grief is a part of life. That day, I began to understand that growing up meant learning to carry both joy and sorrow.

As the eldest child, responsibility came early. I learned to care for my younger siblings, to help my mother with chores, to be a second pair of hands and eyes in a busy household. At first, these tasks felt like burdens, interruptions to my play and dreams. But over time, I came to see them as acts of love—a way to contribute, to belong, to prove my worth.

I remember the pride I felt when my mother trusted me to cook a meal on my own, and when my father praised me for helping in the fields. These moments taught me the value of hard work, the satisfaction of a job well done. They also taught me that leadership is not about giving orders, but about serving others.

There were times when I resented the weight of expectation, when I longed for the freedom I saw in my friends' lives. But I also knew that my family depended on me, and that my actions mattered. This sense of purpose became a guiding force as I navigated the challenges of adolescence.

The transition from childhood to adolescence was marked by a growing awareness of the world's injustices. I began to notice the disparities between rich and poor, the way some children went to school while others like me stayed home to work. I saw girls my age forced into early marriages, their dreams sacrificed on the altar of tradition. I heard stories of trafficking, of children taken from their families and lost to the darkness. Some lives were unaccounted, no news about them. I watched as families wailed in agony.

These realisations were painful, but they sparked a fire in me—a desire to fight for justice, to use my voice for those who could not speak. I began to ask questions, to challenge assumptions, to dream of a world where every child could be safe and free. This awakening was both a burden and a blessing, for it gave my life a sense of mission that would shape my choices for years to come.

Education became my passport to a wider world. My parents, especially my mother, believed deeply in the power of learning. She made countless sacrifices to ensure I could attend school, even when money was tight and the future uncertain. I threw myself into my studies, determined to honor her efforts and to carve out a different path for myself.

School was both a refuge and a crucible. I loved the challenge of new ideas, the thrill of discovery, and the friendships that blossomed in the classroom. But it was also a place where I learned hard lessons—about competition, jealousy, and the pain of failure. There were teachers who inspired me, and others who tried to break my spirit. Each experience, good or bad, became a stepping stone on my journey to adulthood.

One turning point came when my Uncle visited during the festive season. Before his return, he took me along to the city, promising my mother I will be attending a prestigious School in the city. it meant leaving home and facing the world as it is. The transition was difficult—I struggled with homesickness, loneliness, and the pressure to succeed. But I also discovered reserves of strength and resilience I didn't know I had.

Adolescence is a time of questioning, of searching for meaning and identity. For me, faith was both an anchor and a source of conflict. I had grown up in a home where prayer was as natural as breathing, where God was a constant presence. But as I encountered new ideas and faced new challenges, I began to wrestle with doubt.

There were moments when I felt abandoned by God, when my prayers seemed to go unanswered, when the weight of suffering threatened to crush my spirit. But there were also moments of grace—unexpected kindnesses, small miracles, the quiet assurance that I was not alone. Over time, my faith deepened, becoming less about rules and rituals and more about a relationship with God, trust in his unfailing arms, and hope in his promises.

One of the most significant realisations of my coming of age was that faith is not the absence of doubt, but the courage to believe in spite of it. This insight has sustained me through many storms, and continues to shape my worldview today.

A coming-of-age story is not complete without its share of pain. For me, the darkest chapter was the experience with trafficking—a violation that shattered my innocence and forced me to grow up far too soon. I have written about this before, and the details are etched into my memory with painful clarity.

What I want to emphasise here is not the horror of what happened, but the strength I found in surviving it. The decision to escape, to fight for my freedom, was the most important turning point of my life. It was a moment of terrifying clarity—a realisation that I deserved better, that I was not defined by what had been done to me. I knew testimony is in being alive.

The journey to healing was long and difficult. I struggled with shame, fear, self-doubt and worth. But each day, I chose to keep going, to reclaim my life one step at a time. I learned to trust again, to hope again, and to believe that my story could have a different ending.

Surviving trauma gave me a new sense of purpose. I realised that my story could be a source of hope for others, that my pain could be transformed into power. I began to speak out, to share my experiences, to advocate for victims and survivors. This was not an easy path—there were times when I wanted to hide, to forget, to pretend that nothing had happened. But I knew that silence was a form of complicity, and that my voice could make a difference.

Writing became both therapy and mission. Each word was an act of defiance, a refusal to be silenced. I discovered that vulnerability is a form of strength, which sharing my truth could inspire others to do the same. This realisation was a key turning point in my journey to adulthood.

Another defining aspect of coming of age was learning to love and to lose. My first crush, my first heartbreak, the friendships that blossomed and faded—each taught me something about myself and about the nature of relationships. This is another topic on its own. I have this to say - when you get into a relationship, find out where the other person has placed you. Ask yourself – does this person take me the way I took him/her. I learned that love is both joy and risk, that it requires courage, honesty, and the willingness to be hurt.

The loss of my father was a profound turning point. His death left a void that could never be filled, but it also taught me the importance of cherishing those we love, of saying what needs to be said, of doing what needs to be done, of living with no regrets. Grief became a teacher, showing me the fragility of life and the necessity of forgiveness. I learnt the necessity of caring for our parents the best way we can while they are still living.

Becoming a mother was perhaps the most significant rite of passage in my journey to adulthood. The birth of my children was a miracle, a source of indescribable joy and responsibility. Motherhood forced me to grow in ways I could never have imagined—it demanded patience, sacrifice, and a kind of love that is both fierce and tender.

Balancing motherhood with education and career was a constant challenge. There were days when I doubted myself, when exhaustion threatened to overwhelm me. But each milestone—my graduation, my first job, my children's first steps—was a testament to my resilience and determination.

Motherhood also deepened my faith, reminding me daily of the miracles that surround us. My children are my greatest teachers, my greatest motivation, and the clearest evidence that hope is never wasted.

Looking back, I see that my coming of age was shaped by a series of key decisions:

- Choosing to pursue education, even when it meant sacrifice and struggle.
- Deciding to escape from trafficking, to fight for my freedom and my future.
- Choosing to forgive—not just those who hurt me, but myself.
- Deciding to speak out, to use my story as a tool for healing and change.
- Choosing to love, to risk vulnerability, to build a family and a life rooted in faith and hope.

Each decision was a turning point, a step toward the woman I am becoming. Each realization—about the nature of suffering, the power of faith, the importance of community—has shaped my worldview and my sense of purpose.

Coming of age is not a destination, but a journey. I am still learning, still growing, still discovering new facets of myself and the world around me. There are days when I feel strong and confident, and days when I am overwhelmed by doubt and fear. But I know now that this is what it means to be human—to live with uncertainty, to embrace both the light and the darkness.

I am grateful for every lesson, every challenge, every blessing. I am proud of the woman I have become, and hopeful for the woman I am still becoming.

As I stand on the threshold of the next chapter of my life, I do so with gratitude and hope. I know that there will be more challenges, more losses, and more moments of doubt. But I also know that I am not alone—that I am surrounded by love, guided by faith, and strengthened by the lessons of my past.

Coming of age has taught me that life is a gift, that every day is an opportunity to grow, to love, to make a difference. I embrace the future with open hands and an open heart, trusting that the best is yet to come.

Chapter 25

Looking Back, Moving Forward

As I sit down to write this final chapter, I am filled with a deep sense of gratitude and awe. To look back on my journey is to witness a tapestry woven with threads of pain and joy, loss and triumph, faith and doubt. Each chapter of my life—every struggle, every victory, every moment of uncertainty—has brought me to this point. And as I reflect, I see not just where I have been, but also where I am going.

My life began in the heart of Anambra State, Nigeria, in a family that cherished tradition, faith, and community. I was born in a year of abundance, my arrival celebrated with songs and stories that have followed me ever since. My names—Roseline, Chinasa, Egodi, Unoego, Nwaogalanyi (Daughter of a rich man)—carry the weight of history and hope. They remind me of who I am and where I come from: a child of answered prayers, a symbol of blessing, a living testimony to God's faithfulness.

Growing up, I was surrounded by love, but also by responsibility and the harsh reality of life that later unfold. As the first child, I learned early that my actions mattered—not just for myself, but for my siblings, my parents, and my community. My mother's hands taught me the value of hard work; my father's songs taught me the power of joy. Our home was filled with laughter, shared meals, and the rhythms of daily life. These memories are the foundation upon which I have built everything else.

But life is never simple. The innocence of childhood gave way to the complexities of adolescence and the harsh realities of adulthood. I encountered injustice, loss, and trauma—most painfully, my experience with trafficking. That chapter of my life was marked by fear and despair, by a sense of powerlessness that threatened to consume me. Yet even in the darkest moments, I found glimmers of hope: a kind word, a helping hand, a prayer whispered in the night.

If there is one thread that runs through every chapter of my story, it is faith. Faith in God, faith in the possibility of a better tomorrow, faith in the power of love and forgiveness. My faith has been tested—by grief, by betrayal, by the long road to healing—but it has never been broken.

I have learned that faith is not the absence of doubt, but the courage to believe in spite of it. It is the willingness to trust that God is working, even when I cannot see the outcome. It is the quiet assurance that every trial has a purpose, every tear is counted, and every prayer is heard.

Prayer has been my lifeline. In moments of despair, I have cried out to God, sometimes with words, sometimes with only tears. And time after time, I have experienced miracles—some dramatic, some so subtle that I only recognized them in hindsight. I have seen doors open, obstacles removed, and hearts changed. I have learned to wait, to hope, and to trust that God's timing is always perfect. Trust God's timing. He is always on time. Always remember that nothing takes God by surprise. Every journey of our lives was destined before our existence.

Family has been both my anchor and my inspiration. My mother's sacrifices made my education possible; their love gave me the confidence to dream. My husband has been my companion, and confidants, and my greatest supporter. The lessons I learned at home—about kindness, resilience, and the importance of community—have shaped every decision I have made.

Becoming a mother myself, was a turning point. My children are my greatest blessing and my greatest responsibility. They remind me daily of the power of unconditional love, the importance of patience, and the joy of discovery. Every milestone—first steps, first words, first days of school—has been a miracle. They are my motivation to keep striving, to keep growing, to keep believing in the possibility of a better world.

My husband has been my partner in every sense. Together, we have navigated the challenges of marriage, parenthood, and career. His support has been unwavering, his love a source of strength. Our home is not perfect—no home is—but it is filled with laughter, faith, and the determination to build a legacy for our children.

For many years, I struggled to find meaning in my suffering. Why did I have to endure so much pain and suffering? Why was my path so different and difficult? Why me amongst all my siblings? Why did God allow things happen the way they did? Unfortunately, no one had the right answer. I lived without answers for years until I began to read and meditate on the word of God. Jeremiah 1:5 had the answers I have been searching for all these years.

Jeremiah 1:5 says "before I formed you in the womb I knew you, before you were born I set you apart and I ordained you....". This scripture is deeper than ordinary eyes can see. I have encounter each time I meditate on this scripture. It was when I began to heal that I realized God knew my story beforehand. He knows me more than I know myself. The question I keep asking was, can I be a source of hope for others. It has all been written before their manifestations. My pain could be transformed into power, my scars into testimony.

Writing this book has been an act of courage and vulnerability. It has forced me to revisit old wounds, to confront memories I would rather forget. But it has also been a process of liberation—a way to reclaim my story, to speak truth to power, to offer encouragement to those who are still trapped in darkness.

I write for every survivor who feels alone, for every child who dreams of freedom, for every parent who prays for a better future. I write to say: you are not alone. Your story matters. Your pain is real, but so is your strength. There is hope, even when it seems impossible.

As I look back, I see that my journey has been shaped by three major themes: faith, family, and purpose.

Faith has been my compass, guiding me through uncertainty and fear. It has given me the strength to persevere, the courage to forgive, and the hope to dream.

Family has been my foundation, grounding me in love and tradition. It has taught me the value of sacrifice, the importance of community, and the power of legacy.

Purpose has been my motivation, turning my pain into a mission. It has inspired me to speak out, to advocate for change, to use my story as a tool for healing and empowerment.

These themes are not separate threads, but a single braid—each one strengthening the others, each one essential to the whole.

Looking back, I have learned many lessons—some easy, some hard. I have learned that life is unpredictable, that suffering is inevitable, but that joy is always possible. I have learned that forgiveness is not a gift to others, but a gift to myself. I have learned that hope is a choice, not a feeling, and that faith is a journey, not a destination.

I have learned to cherish the ordinary moments: a shared meal, a song sung in church, a child's laughter, a quiet morning spent in prayer. These are the miracles that sustain me, the reminders that life is beautiful, even in its brokenness.

I have learned that my worth is not defined by my past, but by my resilience, my compassion, and my willingness to keep moving forward. Keeping my eyes focused on the purpose I was created for.

As I close this chapter, I do so with a sense of anticipation. My journey is not over. There are still battles to fight, dreams to pursue, purpose to discover, and stories to tell. I am committed to using my voice for good—to advocate for survivors, to educate others about the realities of trafficking, to support families and communities in need.

I plan to continue my education, to grow in my profession, to be the best mother, wife, and friend I can be. I want to write more books, to share more stories, to leave a legacy of hope and healing for future generations.

Most importantly, I want to live each day with gratitude—with open hands and an open heart, ready to receive whatever blessings and challenges come my way.

If you are reading this, know that you are part of my story. Your willingness to listen, to learn, to empathize, is a gift. I hope that my journey has inspired you to reflect on your own life, to cherish your loved ones, to hold fast to your faith, and to pursue your purpose with courage and determination.

If you are struggling, know that you are not alone. There is always hope. There is always a way forward. Your story is not over. The pain you feel today can become the strength you need tomorrow.

If you are a survivor, I honor your courage. Your scars are a testament to your strength. Your voice matters. Your life has meaning.

As I move forward, I carry with me the lessons of the past and the hopes of the future. I am grateful for every person who has walked this path with me—my family, my friends, my mentors, my readers. You have been my companions, my encouragers, and my inspiration.

I do not know what the future holds, but I know who holds the future. My faith in God remains unshaken, my love for my family unwavering, and my commitment to my purpose undiminished.

There will be new challenges, new joys, and new miracles. There will be days of doubt and days of triumph. But through it all, I will keep moving forward—one step at a time, one story at a time, one act of love at a time.

Looking back, I see a life marked by struggle and redemption, by loss and abundance, by fear and faith. I see a woman who refused to be defined by her circumstances, who chose hope over despair, who found meaning in the midst of suffering.

Moving forward, I am determined to live with intention—to love deeply, to serve faithfully, and to pursue justice and mercy, to leave the world better than I found it.

This is my story. This is my legacy. And this is only the beginning.

Q&A Section

Understanding My Story

Q1: Why did you choose to stay silent about Madam Gold not being your stepmother for so long?

A: I was terrified. Madam Gold had threatened me repeatedly, warning that if I revealed the truth, I would be blamed, punished, or even removed from school. I had no support system I trusted fully, and fear kept me silent.

Q2: How did you cope with the constant physical and emotional abuse?

A: I clung to school and education. Going to school gave me a sense of normalcy and a glimpse of a life outside Madam Gold's control. I also found support in people like Flora, who offered small acts of kindness that became lifelines.

Q3: How did you finally reconnect with your mother?

A: With Flora's help, I went through the phone numbers Madam Gold had forced me to record. After calling many numbers, I reached Clem, who helped me contact my mother. Hearing her voice after so many years was overwhelming and deeply healing.

Q4: How did it feel to receive your baptismal and birth certificates?

A: It was a moment of reclaiming my identity. Those documents proved who I truly was and reminded me that despite all the control and lies, I still had a personal history and family who loved me.

Q5: How did the police involvement affect your life?

A: The police provided protection and created a way out, but it also reinforced fear, as Madam Gold threatened me afterward. It taught me that speaking out was necessary for safety, even when I was terrified of the consequences.

Q6: What kept you going despite all the abuse?

A: My education, the hope of reconnecting with my family, and small acts of kindness from people like Flora. Each day I survived felt like a small victory, and the idea of a better future kept me moving forward.

Q7: What message would you like readers to take away from your story?

A: That even in the darkest situations, hope and courage can carry you through. Speaking out, seeking help, and holding on to your identity are powerful steps toward reclaiming your life.

Author Biography

Roseline Chinasa Oiwoh is a Nigerian-born survivor, author, and fierce advocate based in London, UK. Her debut, *Scars of Silence*, exposes the brutal truth of human trafficking with unflinching courage. As a committed member of AFRUCA (Africans Unite Against Child Abuse), a UK-based organization dedicated to protecting and empowering vulnerable African children and families, Roseline transforms her trauma into a battle cry for justice and healing. Through her words, she breaks the silence, challenges stigma, and empowers survivors to reclaim their power. Her mission is clear: to ignite change, give voice to the voiceless, and ensure no survivor suffers alone.

"Together, we can break the chains of silence, restore hope, and build a future where every survivor's voice is heard and honored."

Contact the Author:

Connect with on Facebook: Roseline C. Oiwoh

Or email: roselineoiwoh@gmail.com

Resources & Support

-National Human Trafficking Hotline (US): 1-888-373-7888 | humantraffickinghotline.org

-International Organisation for Migration (IOM): www.iom.int

-AFRUCA (Africans Unite Against Child Abuse): www.afruca.org

-Polaris Project: polarisproject.org

If you or someone you know needs help, these organizations offer vital resources and support.

Thank you.

www.ingramcontent.com/pod-product-compliance
Lightning Source LLC
Chambersburg PA
CBHW061759070526
44586CB00023B/2632